New Directions for
Student Services

Elizabeth J. Whitt
EDITOR-IN-CHIEF

John H. Schuh
ASSOCIATE EDITOR

The State of the College Union: Contemporary Issues and Trends

Tamara Yakaboski
Danielle M. De Sawal
EDITORS

Number 145 • Spring 2014
Jossey-Bass
San Francisco

THE STATE OF THE COLLEGE UNION: CONTEMPORARY ISSUES AND TRENDS
Tamara Yakaboski, Danielle M. De Sawal (eds.)
New Directions for Student Services, no. 145

Elizabeth J. Whitt, Editor-in-Chief
John H. Schuh, Associate Editor

NEW DIRECTIONS FOR STUDENT SERVICES (ISSN 0164-7970, e-ISSN 1536-0695) is part of The Jossey-Bass Higher and Adult Education Series and is published quarterly by Wiley Subscription Services, Inc., A Wiley Company, at Jossey-Bass, One Montgomery Street, Suite 1200, San Francisco, CA 94104-4594. POSTMASTER: Send address changes to New Directions for Student Services, Jossey-Bass, One Montgomery Street, Suite 1200, San Francisco, CA 94104-4594.

New Directions for Student Services is indexed in CIJE: Current Index to Journals in Education (ERIC), Contents Pages in Education (T&F), Current Abstracts (EBSCO), Education Index /Abstracts (H.W. Wilson), Educational Research Abstracts Online (T&F), ERIC Database (Education Resources Information Center), and Higher Education Abstracts (Claremont Graduate University).

Microfilm copies of issues and articles are available in 16 mm and 35 mm, as well as microfiche in 105mm, through University Microfilms Inc., 300 North Zeeb Road, Ann Arbor, Michigan 48106-1346.

SUBSCRIPTIONS cost $89 for individuals in the U.S., Canada, and Mexico, and $113 in the rest of the world for print only; $89 in all regions for electronic only; and $98 in the U.S., Canada, and Mexico for combined print and electronic; and $122 for combined print and electronic in the rest of the world. Institutional print only subscriptions are $311 in the U.S., $351 in Canada and Mexico, and $385 in the rest of the world; electronic only subscriptions are $311 in all regions; and combined print and electronic subscriptions are $357 in the U.S., $397 in Canada and Mexico, and $431 in the rest of the world.

EDITORIAL CORRESPONDENCE should be sent to the Editor-in-Chief, Elizabeth J. Whitt, University of California Merced, 5200 North Lake Rd. Merced, CA 95343.

www.josseybass.com

CONTENTS

EDITORS' NOTES

College unions have been established as the "living room of the college campus" (Association of College Unions International, 1996, para. 4) and the "community center of the college, for all members of the college family—students, faculty, administration, alumni, and guests" (Packwood, 1977, p. 180). College unions also serve as learning laboratories for students through employment, engagement, and leadership opportunities. Senior-level administrators and college union professionals need to be aware of the trends and issues facing college unions in the 21st century. This volume addresses those trends and offers suggestions for research and practice in college unions.

In 2014, the Association of College Unions International (ACUI) celebrates its 100th anniversary, thus making it one of the oldest student affairs professional associations. The National Association of Student Unions—as it was first known—hosted its first conference at The Ohio State University with a combination of college union personnel, faculty, and students (Berry & Looman, 1960). Seeking to understand the commonalities and differences that existed in college unions across types of institutions, the association began to document and record effective practices and track trends in the work of college union practitioners. Milani and Johnston (1992) noted that the evolution of the "college union movement and that of the Association of College Unions-International (ACU-I) are inseparable" (p. 1).

College union ideals, which reflect the distinct purpose and rationale of a college union, have been part of the landscape of higher education since the Harvard Union was established in 1832 at Harvard College and Houston Hall was built in 1896 at the University of Pennsylvania (Berry & Looman, 1960; Milani, Eakin, & Brattain, 1992).

As professional staff examine the current trends and issues facing college unions, they should look to the next 100 years to ensure that the college union continues to have a dominant role in creating community and engagement. This volume draws on the expertise and experiences of college union professionals and student affairs scholars to address the current state and forecast the future of college unions in higher education. Porter Butts (1971) defined the college union idea through a historical journey that highlighted the growth and challenges faced by professionals working on college campuses. The current state of higher education requires college union professionals to understand not only the history of the college union but also how their work can advance the role of the college from a diverse perspective.

Current handbooks about student affairs and the functional areas of the field do not truly address the unique work and organizational design of the college union on today's campus. Although college unions often are

NEW DIRECTIONS FOR STUDENT SERVICES, no. 145, Spring 2014 © 2014 Wiley Periodicals, Inc.
Published online in Wiley Online Library (wileyonlinelibrary.com) • DOI: 10.1002/ss.20074

mentioned in relation to auxiliary services and student programming on college campuses, college unions are a unique student service. Milani and Johnston (1992) provided the most recent *New Directions* monograph focused on what college unions would look like in the year 2000. The 100th anniversary of ACUI and the lack of recent literature on the state of college unions provide an opportunity to reflect on the future of this area of student affairs.

Tamara Yakaboski
Danielle M. De Sawal
Editors

References

Association of College Unions International. (1996). *Role of the college union.* Retrieved from http://www.acui.org/content.aspx?menu_id=30&id=296

Berry, C. A., & Looman, A. R. (Eds.). (1960). *College unions...year fifty.* Ithaca, NY: Association of College Unions.

Butts, P. (1971). *The college union idea.* Stanford, CA: Association of College Unions International.

Milani, T. E., Eakin, J. T., & Brattain, W. E. (1992). The role of the college union and the future. In T. E. Milani & J. W. Johnston (Eds.), *New Directions for Student Services: No. 58. The college union in the year 2000* (pp. 3–10). San Francisco, CA: Jossey-Bass.

Milani, T. E., & Johnston, J. W. (Eds.). (1992). *New Directions for Student Services: No. 58. The college union in the year 2000.* San Francisco, CA: Jossey-Bass.

Packwood, W. T. (Ed.). (1977). *College student personnel services.* Springfield, IL: Charles C. Thomas Publisher.

TAMARA YAKABOSKI is an associate professor in Higher Education and Student Affairs Leadership at the University of Northern Colorado.

DANIELLE M. DE SAWAL is a clinical associate professor and coordinator of the Higher Education and Student Affairs master's program at Indiana University.

1

This chapter explores the state of college unions on today's campuses.

Revisiting the Role of the College Union

Robert M. Rouzer, Danielle M. De Sawal, Tamara Yakaboski

The state of college unions in the 21st century provides an opportunity for college union professionals and higher education administrators to reflect on its rich history and strategize for the future. Referred to as the "living room of the college campus" (Association of College Unions International, 1996, para. 4) and the "community center of the college, for all members of the college family—students, faculty, administration, alumni, and guests" (Packwood, 1977, p. 180), the historical roots of college unions are grounded in student involvement and recreation. The development of debating societies and focus on leisure time recreation prior to WWII evolved to focus on how college unions played a role in creating community on campus for faculty, staff, and students to gather for both social and intellectual pursuits. Professionals associated with the Association of College Unions International (ACUI) established *The Role of the College Union* (ACUI, 1996) to guide their professional practice in the field. The current state of college unions is best understood by evaluating how the role of college unions on higher education campuses translates into practice.

The core of *The Role of the College Union* (ACUI, 1996) statement is the idea that a college union is the campus leader in building community. It is difficult to find literature that provides a common definition for campus community, and Wiley (2003) noted that the concept of community building on college campuses is an elusive goal for higher education. In Ernest Boyer's (1990) seminal work, *Campus Life: In Search of Community*, he outlined the characteristics necessary for a college campus to establish a common community. On some campuses, the college union was the first campus facility that was neither a place for academic classrooms nor a student residence. As a result, it is easy to see how college unions became known as the "living room" of the campus. College unions created the conditions for faculty and students to gather in what could be considered a neutral space for both social and intellectual interactions. The physical design of the college union building invited casual conversations and interactions in a more intimate setting than a lecture hall or a dormitory.

NEW DIRECTIONS FOR STUDENT SERVICES, no. 145, Spring 2014 © 2014 Wiley Periodicals, Inc.
Published online in Wiley Online Library (wileyonlinelibrary.com) • DOI: 10.1002/ss.20075

Historically, those working in college unions could link their work to a physical structure on campus. The college union building was an important part of both the institutions landscape and how professionals within that facility identified with their work. Porter Butts (1971) gathered personal reflections, speeches, and writings on college unions to identify themes in how professionals approached their work in these facilities, which became known as *The College Union Idea*. Originally conceptualized to illustrate the seamless environment college unions provided in regard to both a physical space on campus and as a learning-centered environment, *The College Union Idea* provided context for the work of professionals in college unions.

The growth of fusion spaces or multiuse space has resulted in auxiliary challenges related to a need for traditional gathering location and the separation of functions within the facilities (Rullman, Strong, Farley, Keegan, & White, 2008). A shift has emerged and many higher education organizations are seeing a separation between the programming and the operational components associated with college unions, dismantling the once strong connection that existed between the space and intellectual dialogue. Maintaining separate programming and operations functions could be a threat to the foundational ideals of student-centered community on which college unions were built.

Physical space on campus provides "structure to social institutions, durability to social networks, persistence to behavior patterns" (Gieryn, 2002, p. 35). Although college union ideals surrounding the creation of community do not have to be tied to one specific space, they are linked to the facilities present on campus. Those facilities create the context for the environmental conditions established for social and intellectual dialogue. In a recent report on physical space in higher education, it was noted that "flexibility, adaptability, responsiveness, and a sense of ownership may be more important than the architecture, tradition, or permanence of most campus facilities" (Rullman & van den Kieboom, 2012, p. 23).

The history of college unions illustrates how the role of space on campus has evolved to showcase campus services, establish new sources of revenue, and dedicate space for informal and formal learning. Today, college unions are no longer the only spaces on campus designed to create social and intellectual engagement. Responding to Boyer's (1990) call for the creation of campus community, both student affairs and academic affairs organizations have developed spaces for social and intellectual engagement. Gieryn (2002) noted that "the play of agency and structure happens as we build: we mold buildings, they mold us, we mold them anew..." (p. 65). As higher education administrators examine how campuses create and use space, professionals in college unions need to rethink their role on campus as community builders in the 21st century.

At the same time, college unions struggle between pressures to enhance the overall university's revenue as state funding continues to decrease and college costs increase while maintaining a commitment to student development and engagement and supporting the academic mission of the institution amid changing student demographics and values. These trends have run the risk of encouraging college union professionals to change from viewing students as learners to increasingly describing students as customers or consumers. The shift to a business or customer service model is often incongruent with an educational focus, which measures learning outcomes not customer satisfaction (Davis, 2011). Ultimately, the shift to a business model makes it more challenging for college unions to justify their fit within the academic mission or focus on student development and engagement.

Milani, Eakin, and Brattain (1992) predicted six issues that would have an impact on college unions for the year 2000. Those themes were: (a) more diverse populations, (b) expanded technology and the rate of knowledge change, (c) changes in student values and lifestyles, (d) increased competition for resources, (e) a more volatile political climate, and (f) increased external accountability. A look back twenty years at those predictions and a look forward to the next decade shows that some of those themes will continue to be important, while others have become less so. We examine each of those issues in the following sections.

Changing Student Demographics

College student characteristics have changed over the past twenty years (Renn & Reason, 2013). Of the 21.0 million students enrolled in higher education (National Center for Education Statistics, n.d.), "traditional students are no longer the tradition" (Borden, 2004, p. 10). Since the 1980s, higher education has seen an increase in students from all racial and ethnic backgrounds enrolling in college (The Chronicle of Higher Education, 2012). Changes in the racial composition of the population of the United States and changes in the rates at which members of underrepresented groups are enrolling in higher education have contributed to this increase (Pryor, Hurtado, Saenz, Santos, & Korn, 2007; Snyder & Dillow, 2009).

The average age of students attending college at the undergraduate level is also increasing; approximately 38% of all undergraduates are over the age of 25 (Hess, 2011). Women have been the "stable majority" in higher education since 1979 outpacing men's enrollment (Pryor et al., 2007, p. 4). The number of international students studying in the United States has doubled since 1980 to 3.5% of all students in 2010 (The Chronicle of Higher Education, 2012) with the largest populations from China and India, and noticeable increases from Southeast Asian nations and Saudi Arabia (Institute of International Education, 2012).

Changing student demographics require college union professionals to examine their use of space and programmatic initiatives to remain responsive to the changing student populations. Creating environments that foster spiritual development through prayer and meditation spaces

NEW DIRECTIONS FOR STUDENT SERVICES • DOI: 10.1002/ss

(Sapp, 2013) and establishing locations for lactating mothers (University of Maryland, College Park, n.d.) are examples of how the use of space in college unions has been affected by changes in the student population.

These changes in student demographics also have an impact on how community within college unions can be established. As college enrollments increase and the student population diversifies, so do the services offered on college campuses. Campuses have seen in the last twenty years an increase in the number of ethnic and racial centers on campus, community gathering places within academic and campus residence centers, and offices dedicated to specific student identity populations (e.g., student veterans and LGBT students). Butts (1971) noted in his interpretation of the role of college unions that the growth of student specific organizations on campus risked creating a campus community that could "become insular, withdrawing into themselves, splitting the campus socially" (p. 102). The diversification of the college population on campuses directly impacts the way in which college union professionals are able to create the conditions necessary for community building.

Rhodes (2001) articulated that an educator's "task is to educate citizens of a new society, embracing diversity with confidence rather than escaping from it in cloistered isolation, facing the challenges of disagreement rather than sheltering from them in a capsule of silent indifference" (p. 48). Creating the conditions for community building within college unions will continue to become more complex as access to higher education expands and higher education continues to globalize. It is the role of today's college union professional to stay current on changing student demographics on his or her campus and the specific implications for college unions of those changes.

Technological Expansion

The College Union in the Year 2000 was written before the advent of the World Wide Web, thus Milani et al. (1992) could not foresee the myriad ways that easy access to the Internet would change how individuals and organizations interact with each other and the world in general. Advances in technology and increased access to the Internet have encouraged and even demanded incorporating technology into classroom teaching and university services, thus impacting how students learn and interact with the institution. Nearly 100% of American undergraduate and graduate students ages 18–24 reported using the Internet and over 80% used some form of social media (Smith, Rainie, & Zickuhr, 2011) though not necessarily for academic purposes. And, although many students entering college use and think about technology in ways that previous generations may not understand, not all undergraduates possess sufficient knowledge about how to assess online resources critically (Hargittai, 2010).

NEW DIRECTIONS FOR STUDENT SERVICES • DOI: 10.1002/ss

Research has demonstrated that using technology in the classroom can enhance student learning, engagement, and interactions (National Survey of Student Engagement, 2009), but how can college unions use technology to improve experiential learning outside the classroom? Since incorporating social media, such as Twitter or Facebook, into the classroom may improve peer and faculty engagement and interactions (Junco, Heiberger, & Loken, 2011), college union professionals could use them to create engagement for online and commuting students. The abundance of Internet access provides marketing opportunities for college union professionals as well as opportunities to create new digital spaces for successful engagement and involvement.

Increasingly, courses and instructors are using digital textbooks, thereby changing the nature of campus-based bookstores through electronic textbook rentals or e-books (McDermott, North, Meszaros, Caywood, & Danzell, 2011). Thirty-two percent of all higher education students will take at least one online course and 6.7 million students took an online course in fall 2011 (Allen & Seaman, 2013). Both have implications for the role of college unions in providing course materials for faculty and students.

Technological advances will continue to impact the way college unions will need to respond to changing expectations for services and need for digital engagement. In addition, college union professionals should be prepared to help students use electronic technologies appropriately and ethically.

Students' Changing Lifestyles and Values

Milani et al. (1992) predicted that the "factors that affect [student's lifestyles and values] changes are complex, dynamic, unpredictable, and difficult to measure" (p. 7). Therefore, changes in technology, politics, and the economic climate could threaten college unions' connection to educating students and being a community builder. As the demographics of college students have changed so too has the purpose of attending college and the value of an education. In the most recent Almanac of Higher Education (The Chronicle of Higher Education, 2012), students reported that 72.3% of them view a college education as the means to increase earnings, train for a career (77.6%), or obtain a better job (85.9%). Only 50.3% stated it was to become more cultured. Students' political identities have changed to more students politically identifying themselves as "middle of the road" (47.4%) rather than liberal (27.6%) or conservative (20.7%). The majority of college students believe in keeping abortions legal (60.7%), legalizing marijuana (49.1%), same-sex couples adoption rights (71.3%), undocumented students' access to public education (57%), national health care (60.5%), and that government should address global warming (63.2%; The Chronicle of Higher Education, 2012). These trends present opportunities for college union professionals to diversify programming and educational efforts and be creative in connecting to student groups.

Increased access to, and advancements in, technology and social media have also altered students' lifestyles. Social media have reshaped college student's identities and development in positive and worrisome ways. For example, social networking may be harmfully addictive and lead to increased narcissism (Dalton & Crosby, 2013) and may negatively affect students' sleep habits, self-control and need for immediate responses, and inability to successfully multitask (Grummon, 2013). While technology has improved the quality and effectiveness of higher education, college union professionals should proceed with intentionality and well thought out learning outcomes before using technology to connect with students.

A final lifestyle and values trend causing college union professionals to evaluate their practices, policies, and organizational culture is in relation to the increased attention to students' spirituality, which broadly includes religion and other spiritual practices and belief systems (Kazanjian, 2013). College union professionals need to embrace a more spiritual awareness that requires a new approach to education and intentional community outreach and involvement.

Accountability, Competition for Resources, and the Assessment Movement

In 1992 when *The College Union in the Year 2000* was published, the authors indicated that pressure for colleges and universities to be accountable to institutional, state, and federal entities for a broad range of outcomes, results, and practices was an issue of growing importance. They noted that 35 states had formal policies on assessment for educational institutions (Parnell, 1990) and that needs assessment and outcomes-based assessment must become important components of college union planning and practice. These expectations have persisted and grown in the past 20 years. State and federal legislators and agencies faced with limited financial resources and rapidly growing financial obligations related to public employee pensions and health care costs have reduced funding to both K–12 and higher education and imposed unfunded regulations such as assessment requirements and reporting (Heller, 2004).

In higher education, outcomes-based assessment has become an increasingly important component of the accreditation process for most accrediting agencies (Harcleroad & Eaton, 2005). And while college unions may be funded by tuition, fees, state allocations, gifts, or a combination of these elements, often the funding processes require assessment to demonstrate links to strategic goals and objectives.

Assessment and accountability are also important components in the increasingly challenging competition for campus resources. Ness and Tandberg (2013) found that political variables do influence the distribution of state capital expenditures within higher education. In the coming years, in spite of demonstrated need, it may be difficult to find support for renovations, expansions, or new construction. The shift of college unions to an auxiliary service component on campus has also resulted in the recognition that student fees may be one of the only remaining paths for professionals to explore in regard to expanding financial support. Many college unions will require student fee referenda for financial support of the facility and programs (Brailsford, Turner, & Thompson, 1999). As a result, professionals working in college unions will need to maintain high levels of engagement with the student body to promote support for fee increases.

Conclusion: The Future of College Unions

Berry (1960) predicted that in 2014 college union professionals may find that "Permanent hair cuts may eliminate our barber shops. We may not need coat rooms as plastic domes cover campuses, or even cities. Or maybe it will only rain at night in 2014. Nutritional requirements may be met by multi-purpose pills and reinforced Metrecal. Instead of providing food service we may be refueling strap-on-helicopters. It is difficult to believe that services of some sort won't be needed" (p. 96). Although humorous to read today, the value in Berry's predictions is that it is hard to predict the future of the role of college unions. The specific products or services that may impact college union professional's work are hard to forecast. However, the history of higher education has provided evidence that the student population will change and be impacted by how society evolves. As discussed in later chapters, technology and the racial and ethnic diversification of college campuses have been two of the largest factors that impact college union work on campus. The evolution of college unions to embrace a business model management style altered how union professionals generate revenue and account for resources.

Many questions face college union professionals. What value do college unions provide to students, not just some students, but all students that attend the institution? What value does the union provide to the campus, not just as a glamorous recruiting tool, but as a provider of vital services and space for community and student engagement? College union professionals need to create assessment metrics to demonstrate the value of college union created community. In addition, with respect to online technologies, college union professionals need to identify methods of extending and sustaining the campus community for those students. The two college union functions of providing services and creating conditions for student learning can be connected; however, college union professionals will have to be intentional in their approach to balancing the delivery of services and creating the optimal conditions for learning within the college union.

In the following chapters, college union professionals and higher education scholars focus on how building community via college unions in the 21st century will be impacted by technology, competition for resources and need for fundraising, a continuing changing student population, globalization and the trend to internationalize, and increased external accountability through assessment, evaluation, and research.

References

Allen, I. E., & Seaman, J. (2013). *Change course: Ten years of tracking online education in the United States*. Babson Park, MA: Babson Survey Research Group.

Association of College Unions International. (ACUI). (1996). *Role of the College Union*. Retrieved from http://www.acui.org/content.aspx?menu_id=30& id=296

Berry, C. A. (1960). The next fifty years of college unions. In C. A. Berry & A. R. Looman (Eds.), *College unions...year fifty* (pp. 96–102). Ithaca, NY: Association of College Unions.

Borden, V. M. H. (2004). Accommodating student swirl: When traditional students are no longer the tradition. *Change, 36*(2), 10–17.

Boyer, E. (1990). *Campus life: In search of community*. San Francisco, CA: Jossey-Bass.

Brailsford, P., Turner, J. D., & Thompson, E. (1999). Planning, preparation lead to successful student fee referendums. *ACUI Bulletin*. Retrieved from http://www .programmanagers.com/resources-publications

Butts, P. (1971). *The college union idea*. Stanford, CA: Association of College Unions International.

The Chronicle of Higher Education. (2012). *Almanac of higher education 2012*. Retrieved from http://chronicle.com/article/Almanac-2012-Students /133763/?f-nav

Dalton, J. C., & Crosby, P. C. (2013). Digital identity: How social media is influencing student learning and development in college. *Journal of College and Character, 14*(1), 1–4.

Davis, T. (2011). In this age of consumerism, what are the implications of giving students what they want? Have it your way U. In P. M. Magolda & M. B. Baxter Magolda (Eds.), *Contested issues in student affairs: Diverse perspectives and respectful dialogue* (pp. 85–96). Sterling, VA: Stylus.

Gieryn, T. F. (2002). What buildings do. *Theory and Society, 31*(1), 35–74.

Grummon, P. T. H. (2013). Trends in higher education. *Society for College and University Planning, 9*(1), 1–10.

Harcleroad, F. F., & Eaton, J. S. (2005). The hidden hand: External constituencies and their impact. In P. G. Altbach, R. O. Berdahl, & P. J. Gumport (Eds.), *American higher education in the 21st century: Social, political, and economic challenges* (pp. 253–283). Baltimore, MD: Johns Hopkins University Press.

Hargittai, E. (2010). Digital na(t)ives? Variation in internet skills and uses among members of the "net generation." *Sociological Inquiry, 80*(1), 92–113.

Heller, D. E. (2004). State oversight of academia. In R. G. Ehrenberg (Ed.), *Governing academia: Who is in charge at the Modern University?* (pp. 49–67). Ithaca, NY: Cornell University Press.

Hess, F. (2011). Old school: College's most important trend is the rise of the adult student. *The Atlantic*. Retrieved from http://www.theatlantic.com /business/archive/2011/09/old-school-colleges-most-important-trend-is-the-rise-of -the-adult-student/245823/

Institute of International Education. (2012). Top 25 places of origin of international students, 2010/11-2011/12. *Open doors report on international educational exchange.* Retrieved from http://www.iie.org/en/Research-and-Publications/Open-Doors/Data/International-Students/Leading-Places-of-Origin/2010-12

Junco, R., Heiberger, G., & Loken, E. (2011). The effect of Twitter on college student engagement and grades. *Journal of Computer Assisted Learning, 27*(2), 119–132.

Kazanjian, V. (2013). Spiritual practices on college and university campuses: Understanding the concepts—Broadening the context. *Journal of College and Character, 14*(2), 97–104.

McDermott, J., North, P., Meszaros, G., Caywood, J. A., & Danzell, L. (2011). Exploring the path of bookstore trends. *NACAS College Services, 11*(4), 16–23.

Milani, T. E., Eakin, J. T., & Brattain, W. E. (1992). The role of the college union and the future. In T. E. Milani & J. W. Johnston (Eds.), *New Directions for Student Services: No. 58. The college union in the year 2000* (pp. 3–10). San Francisco, CA: Jossey-Bass.

National Center for Education Statistics. (n.d.). *Fast facts.* Retrieved from http://nces.ed.gov/fastfacts/display.asp?id=98

National Survey of Student Engagement. (2009). *Assessment for improvement: Tracking student engagement over time—annual results.* Bloomington: Indiana University Center for Postsecondary Research.

Ness, E. C., & Tandberg, D. A. (2013). The determinants of state spending on higher education: How capital project funding differs from general fund appropriations. *The Journal of Higher Education, 84*(3), 329–362.

Packwood, W. T. (Ed.). (1977). *College student personnel services.* Springfield, IL: Charles C. Thomas Publisher.

Parnell, D. (1990). *Dateline 2000: The new higher education agenda.* Washington, DC: Community College Press.

Pryor, J. H., Hurtado, S., Saenz, V. B., Santos, J. L., & Korn, W. S. (2007). *The American freshman: Forty year trends, 1966–2006.* Los Angeles, CA: Higher Education Research Institution.

Renn, K. A., & Reason, R. D. (2013). *College students in the United States: Characteristics, experiences, and outcomes.* San Francisco, CA: Jossey-Bass.

Rhodes, F. H. T. (2001). *The creation of the future—The role of the American university.* Ithaca, NY: Cornell University Press.

Rullman, L., Strong, L., Farley, C., Keegan, K., & White, R. (2008). Top 10 auxiliary services trends for 2008: Campus administrators and consultants offer valuable insights. *College Services, 8*(3), 16–19.

Rullman, L., & van den Kieboom, J. (2012). *Physical place on campus: A report on the summit on building community.* Bloomington, IN: Association of College Unions International.

Sapp, C. L. (2013). A great and towering compromise: Religious practice and space at Duke University. *Journal of College and Character, 14*(2), 117–124.

Smith, A., Rainie, L., & Zickuhr, K. (2011). College students and technology. *Pew Internet and American Life Project.* Retrieved from http://www.pewinternet.org/Reports/2011/College-students-and-technology.aspx

Snyder, T. D., & Dillow, S. A. (2009). *Digest of education statistics 2009* (NCES 2010-013). Washington, DC: National Center for Education Statistics.

University of Maryland, College Park. (n.d.). *Lactation/Nursing Mothers' Rooms.* Retrieved from http://studentaffairs.umd.edu/sites/default/files/Lactation-NursingMothersRoomsatUM.pdf

Wiley, L. (Ed.). (2003). Review of W. M. McDonald and Associates, Creating campus community: In search of Ernest Boyer's legacy. *Teachers College Record, 105*(7), 1256–1260.

ROBERT M. ROUZER *is an executive associate director of Campus Auxiliaries and assistant to the vice chancellor for Student Affairs at University of Illinois at Chicago.*

DANIELLE M. DE SAWAL *is a clinical associate professor and coordinator of the Higher Education and Student Affairs master's program at Indiana University.*

TAMARA YAKABOSKI *is an associate professor in Higher Education and Student Affairs Leadership at the University of Northern Colorado.*

NEW DIRECTIONS FOR STUDENT SERVICES • DOI: 10.1002/ss

2

This chapter examines ways to create conditions for inclusivity within college unions.

Serving Diverse Student Populations in College Unions

Willie L. Banks, Jr., Debra L. Hammond, Ebelia Hernandez

College union professionals have always sought to create welcoming and comfortable environments, and when student populations were more homogenous than today, this task was easier to accomplish. Students who were once considered the minority are fast becoming the majority. New, emergent populations are redefining what is meant by campus diversity. Indeed, diversity as used in this chapter refers to higher education's multicultural student population that represents a variety of races/ethnicities, abilities, sexual orientations, immigrant statuses, gender representations, religions, and life experiences.

College unions are in a position to be a central point where institutions can promote inclusion and be a welcoming place for numerous student populations. The aim of this chapter is to provide advice for creating intentional inclusivity. First, we describe the changing demographics of students enrolled in higher education. Then, through the lens of a multicultural organization, we examine four key areas of college unions: (a) physical space, (b) mission statements and diversity statements that promote values of inclusivity, (c) programming, and (d) staffing.

Changing Student Demographics

The racial/ethnic composition of college students has changed dramatically since the last time *New Directions for Student Services* featured a volume on college unions in 1992 (Milani & Johnston, 1992). It is worthwhile to examine the changing national demographics from 1990 to fall 2020 enrollment projections in order to recognize the rate that our communities are becoming more multiculturally diverse. In the 1990s, it may have been well grounded to assume that the "typical" college student was White because more than three fourths of college students identified as White according to national enrollment data (NCES, 2011). White students are projected to decrease to approximately half of all postsecondary students enrolled in 2020

New Directions for Student Services, no. 145, Spring 2014 © 2014 Wiley Periodicals, Inc.
Published online in Wiley Online Library (wileyonlinelibrary.com) • DOI: 10.1002/ss.20076

Figure 2.1. Actual and Projected Percentages (Rounded to the Nearest Whole Number) for Enrollment in All Postsecondary Degree-Granting Institutions, by Race/Ethnicity: Fall 1990 Through Fall 2020.

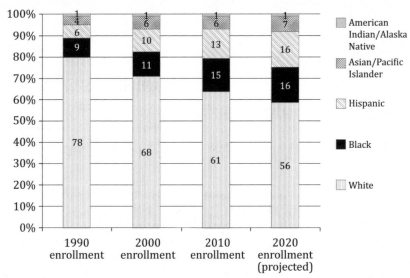

Source: National Center for Education Statistics (NCES). (2011). *Projections of education statistics to 2020*. Retrieved from http://nces.ed.gov/programs/projections/projections2020/tables /table_29.asp?referrer=list

(NCES, 2011). These projections indicate that there will be no overwhelming student majority in the future as the U.S. college population becomes more racially/ethnically heterogeneous (NCES, 2011). Figure 2.1 notes that the trend of increasing racial/ethnic diversity in the United States is well reflected in college enrollment.

A closer look also reveals that while enrollment for Asian/Pacific Islander students and American Indian/Alaskan Native students has remained rather consistent and is projected to remain about the same, the trend of increasing percentages is apparent for Black and Hispanic students. Hispanic students are the fastest growing group, demonstrating a projected 10 percentage point college enrollment growth from 1990 to 2020 (NCES, 2011). While these numbers indicate that more students of color are enrolling in college, Latinos are projected to continue to be severely underrepresented in 2020. Hispanic enrollment is expected to reach 16% despite Latinos comprising approximately 25% of the United States' future population of 18- to 29-year-olds (Santiago & Callan, 2010).

New critical masses of particular student populations have emerged on college campuses that expand the meaning of diversity beyond race/ethnicity to include identities based on lived experiences, nationality, and religion. One such emerging population is student veterans. Approximately 819,200 student veterans were enrolled in institutions of higher education in the United States in 2010 (Hamrick, Rumann, & Associates, 2012). This number is expected to rise in the coming years as the United States continues to withdraw forces overseas. The exact number of student veterans is difficult to determine because the numbers reported by institutions only include those who self-disclose their status to their institution, and higher education institutions have only begun to include them in their statistics. In addition, the federal government also has difficulty in acquiring a more accurate count because it does not track veterans' postsecondary enrollment and not all student veterans currently enrolled use their GI Bill benefits (Hamrick et al., 2012).

Though small in numbers, other student populations have been highlighted as part of campus diversity because of their unique needs and/or political issues. For example, attention toward serving international students is increasing as more institutions seek to recruit students globally as Yakaboski and Perozzi reference in Chapter 8. International students have represented between 3.2% and 3.7% of the student population since 2000; and their numbers have steadily increased to more than 760,000 for the 2011–2012 academic year (Institute of International Education, 2013). In regard to religious diversity, Muslim students represent about 1% of all undergraduates (Higher Education Research Institute, n.d.), but they have become a highly visible group due to incidents of discrimination that have drawn national attention (Hawley, 2012). Another minority group that has become more visible due to discrimination, activism, and national politics regarding marriage equality are lesbian, bisexual, gay, and transgender (LBGT) college students. Campus Pride, an advocacy group aimed at creating a safer college environment for LBGT students (Campus Pride, n.d.), has ranked colleges and universities across the country on their LBGT-friendly campus climate to help institutions assess their level of inclusive programs, policies, and services (Campus Pride Index, n.d.).

Working toward inclusivity requires college union professionals to recognize these and other populations too numerous to review here. Students from historically underrepresented groups have diverse needs and attitudes about college unions. Research indicates that such students (Webster & Sedlacek, 1982) and newcomers to the university environment (e.g., first semester students; Mallinckrodt & Sedlacek, 1985) use college unions more than majority White students. Black students, in particular, may have difficulty in adjusting to the campus climate in predominantly White institutions and may need to attend to nonacademic needs before they can concentrate on academic ones (Mallinckrodt & Sedlacek, 1985). Thus, they may use college unions as places to find community and build a social network.

NEW DIRECTIONS FOR STUDENT SERVICES • DOI: 10.1002/ss

Becoming Intentionally Inclusive in College Unions

College unions have been and will continue to be challenged to create environments that are inclusive, encompassing, and representative of the cultures and communities within higher education institutions. Serving today's students from groups historically underrepresented in higher education requires intentionality. Attention to this trend of increasing diversity is not new as Torres, Howard-Hamilton, & Cooper (2003) noted, "for all diverse groups to feel included, expressions of their own cultural identity—not just the expressions of the majority culture—should be seen on campus" (p. 84).

Professionals working in college unions have a history of being proactive in creating a welcoming campus community for all students through both programming efforts and building design. In 1990, the changing student population was noted among six key trends in the Association of College Unions International's (ACUI) *Task Force 2000 Final Report*, which led to the statement, "the college union must be the multicultural community center for the campus" (Milani, Eakin, & Brattain, 1992, p. 6). Professionals in college unions (ACUI, 2008, para. 4) reaffirmed their commitment to inclusivity and multiculturalism, through ACUI, by issuing a statement that included four beliefs that can be used as a guide for institutions:

1. Systematic acts of inclusion at all levels.
2. Purposeful and authentic communication across cultural lives.
3. Constant re-examination of structures, programs, and services for inclusiveness.
4. Removal of all barriers that prevent members from pursuing their affiliation in a manner consistent with their own experiences.

These beliefs provide a starting point for college union professionals to examine the structure of their organization and to facilitate services and programs that support inclusivity.

Defining and Assessing the Multicultural Organization

LeNorman Strong (1986), who is a former president of ACUI, developed a statement that provided a definition of a multicultural organization, which may serve as a guide for professionals working in college unions who are making an intentional commitment to serving today's diverse student populations. Strong (1986) focused on an organization that is sensitive to a variety of cultures, committed and purposeful about making change, inclusive in its organizational makeup and physical structures, and authentic when addressing challenges.

NEW DIRECTIONS FOR STUDENT SERVICES • DOI: 10.1002/ss

Using Strong's (1986) definition of a multicultural organization professionals working in college unions can assess how they are intentional in promoting inclusivity as well as how today's diverse student population uses college union environments. The following questions may guide professionals during this assessment process:

- *Organizational documents that promote inclusion.* Does the college union's mission statement and values espouse a commitment to diversity? Is the language used in the college union's policies written to promote inclusiveness and sensitivity and reduce oppression?
- *Organizational elements displaying inclusion.* Does the college union display art that depicts elements of a diverse student population? Does the college union have artifacts, such as flags, words, cultural icons, and symbolism, that represent diverse cultures and communities? Does the college union have "inclusive hot spots," that is, areas in the facility where historically underrepresented students may congregate and feel comfortable?
- *Membership.* Does the college union have diverse representation on its governing, advisory, and programming boards? Is the professional staff reflective of the campus demographics?
- *Programs and services.* Does the college union produce or cosponsor programs and services that are multicultural and inviting to a variety of student populations? Does the college union encourage and/or reward programs and services for purposefully seeking opportunities to collaborate with others?
- *Access and accommodations.* Is the college union accessible to students with differing levels of ability? Is the college union website compliant with the Americans with Disabilities Act (ADA)? Are accommodations planned in advance to allow those with disabilities to more fully participate in the programs and services offered in the college union?
- *Sensitivity training and development.* Are professionals working in the college union regularly trained to understand and navigate the complexities of a multicultural campus environment? Does the college union offer programs that seek to sensitize and educate others on campus about multicultural issues, particularly those who may be in the majority?
- *Assessment and authenticity.* Does the college union conduct focus groups or other forms of assessments with diverse groups to evaluate college union environments in terms of inclusiveness and comfort? Is the college union perceived as being open to challenge and change by being willing to listen to and perhaps change policies, procedures, and practices based on diverse points of view? Do professionals working in the college union act on their stated commitments?

Failure to continuously ask these types of questions challenges the potential for college unions to be community centers that serve *all* students.

Torres et al. (2003) stated, "the notion that everyone should just 'fit in' is one entrenched in assimilation rather than respect for diversity" (p. 84). Professionals in college unions need to consider critical issues surrounding diversity expression in the physical space, college union mission statement, and programming initiatives in developing an intentionally inclusive, multicultural organization.

Diversity Expression in Physical Space

Physical spaces communicate inclusion or exclusion, interest or disinterest, and attention or alienation. Several theoretical models, including Schlossberg's (1989) mattering and marginality and Astin's (1999) involvement theory, provide constructs to examine how physical places are critical in building community and positively impact the sense of belonging and engagement for historically underrepresented students (Banning & Bartels, 1997; Harper & Quaye, 2009) in college unions and campuses in general. Transforming a physical space into one that creates the conditions necessary to build community requires "places...that exhibit high levels of human engagement and are imbued with evidence of human-to-human mutuality, psychological safety and refuge, and a strong sense of individual and group ownership" (Rullman & van den Kieboom, 2012, p. 5). Although inclusion is not explicitly indicated in this statement, it conveys a sense of belonging and inclusiveness in college unions that are important to today's diverse student population.

There are a number of college union facilities and programs across the United States that have made great strides in serving diverse populations through their facilities. The Davis Center at the University of Vermont is an exemplar of inclusion providing gender-neutral restroom facilities on each of the four floors, utilizing universal design principles for accessibility to physical spaces, installing a loop hearing system in the multipurpose spaces, and providing a diversity and equity lounge and office space within the facility (University of Vermont, n.d.). These features convey a message to students that their needs have been anticipated and that the institution has made commitments of time, effort, and resources to make them feel comfortable at the Davis Center.

Strange and Banning (2001) noted that the model of the campus ecology and particularly the concept of territoriality are critical in defining and developing multicultural learning environments while Rullman and van den Kieboom (2012) indicated the importance of places of "refuge" for students on campus. Many college union facilities house cultural centers that have the unique ability to create environments that are known to be territorialities, which means that students establish a sense of ownership and control over a physical space in which they identify (Strange & Banning, 2001). Examples of this type of implied ownership and control include the University Student Union (USU) at California State University, Northridge.

The USU sponsors and funds two centers to serve diverse and important emerging segments of the campus community: (a) the Pride Center for lesbian, gay, bisexual, transgender, queer, and questioning students and allies and (b) the Veterans Resource Center for veterans and their dependents. College union facilities have creatively used space to convey a sense of belonging and validation from those cultures while also providing clear messaging to the broader campus community of the value and worth of these populations.

Art and artifacts also affect how students view themselves on campus. Banning and Bartels (1997) found that four categories of physical artifacts—art, signs, graffiti, and architecture—convey important messages about multiculturalism on campus and in college unions. The Davis Center at the University of Vermont showcases a commitment to serving diverse communities by using various languages that say "welcome" at the information desk and a 20-foot wall of the south lobby of the connecting tunnel that is dedicated to social justice messaging. The USU at California State University, Northridge, features student art work in a variety of mediums that highlight diversity, and "peace poles," which are physical structures that state the word "peace" in a variety of languages. These examples provide a context for good practice in using art, artifacts, and the design of physical space to create the conditions that make a diverse student population feel as though their salient identities are part of the campus community.

The College Union Mission Statement

The mission statement of any organization should define the core purpose of that organization. It should denote what is important, who the organization serves, as well as the principles that guide their work. Values and beliefs, written and unwritten, depict fundamental codes of conduct or how a group operates (Kuh, Kinzie, Schuh, Whitt, & Associates, 2005). They also serve as guideposts for decision making and are often how college unions are viewed and evaluated by others.

If serving all students is an important component of a college union, the mission and values must depict that commitment. Principles related to respect, fairness, inclusivity, multiculturalism, diversity, cultural pluralism, and social justice should be highlighted within mission statements. If these values are not specifically referenced, it may convey a message of marginality to today's students of diverse backgrounds (Schlossberg, 1989).

In 1989, Schlossberg asked an important question that is still relevant today: "Can a campus community [within unions] be created that allows all students to find a place of involvement and importance?" (p. 6). For professionals working in college unions who are responsible for building community, this question directly speaks to their ability to develop mission and values statements that project significance and attention to multicultural principles. The college unions that have done this successfully explicitly included keywords to illustrate their values in their mission statements: the University of Vermont's (n.d.) Davis Center ("social justice"), the César Chávez Student Center at San Francisco State University (n.d.; "cultural needs," "value and actively develop diversity"), Portland Community College's (n.d.) University Centers ("hate-free center," "honor humanity," "celebrate difference"), and the University of Houston, Division of Student Affairs (n.d.; "diversity," "intentional inclusion of others"). Kuh et al. (2005) concluded that effective educational practice includes that recognition that a lived mission results in higher-than-predicted graduation scores on the National Survey of Student Engagement (NSSE) and graduation rates.

Programming for Diverse Populations

As the diversity of student populations have increased on college campuses, special attention is needed to address their needs and wants in programming. Research on college student engagement (Kuh, 2003), integration (Tinto, 1993), and involvement (Astin, 1999) points to the connection between students getting involved and higher rates of retention, satisfaction, persistence, and graduation for underrepresented students on college campuses. More specifically, there appears to be a positive connection between the use of a college union for a specific purpose (e.g., outdoor recreation, dances, and concerts) rather than hours spent in the union with increasing student retention (Mallinckrodt & Sedlacek, 2009). Professionals working in college unions are in a position to create the conditions necessary to support the out-of-classroom experiences for students on campus.

Taking an intentional, educational, and engaging approach to programming benefits students and the greater campus community. Careful consideration has to be given to the manner in which professionals in college unions approach programming for diverse populations. Yet, due to limited time and resources, programming in college unions will not meet all the needs of all. Professionals must take into account the audience and intended outcomes to build programs that can address as many students as possible. To that end, three components of student programming within college unions are discussed to consider how to best promote inclusive, effective, and dynamic programming for students from groups historically underrepresented in higher education. Programming within college unions for diverse student populations needs to take into consideration campus collaborations, funding, and professional staffing (Sutton, 2006).

Collaborations.   Typically, programming for diverse populations has fallen to a singular office, center, unit, or committee. Programming is multifaceted, and with shrinking budgets and limited personnel, professionals are challenged to be creative, resourceful, and collaborative. The more successful and impactful programming initiatives occur when the programming is a communal responsibility between students, faculty, staff, and the community at large (Bourassa & Kruger, 2002; Howard-Hamilton, 2000;

Whitt, Nesheim, Guentzel, & Kellogg, 2008). College unions are frequently responsible for providing programming that is considered campus-wide, rather than focused on a specific target population on campus. College union professionals need to collaborate with other offices on-campus to reach the greatest number of students and to maximize resources, especially when programming for diverse populations.

In many ways, programming for a diverse student body takes on a grassroots look and feel because many different groups unite over a common issue or cause. When resources are low and the need to educate is high, offices strategize by collaborating. However, programs are often executed in a more siloed environment without thinking about natural connections to other offices. While some offices may not be able to provide monetary support, many will be able to provide personnel, advertising, printing, or hosting special receptions or lectures. Establishing collaborative relationships with entities on campus that focus on serving diverse student populations (e.g., multicultural centers and academic departments) will also encourage those populations to attend those events.

With the increasing diversity of students enrolling in institutions of higher education, programming will have to address the needs of students who identify themselves in multiple ways that include race, ethnicity, gender, sexual orientation, and other identities they consider salient. Programming for intersecting identities is an opportunity to develop collaborations; however, this type of coalition building requires staff and students to be cognizant of the myriad of differences and similarities between students. This requires college union professionals to think about programs that speak to multiple identities and that can educate the greater community and what types of new collaborations will engage a variety of students.

Funding. As Milani and colleagues (1992) stated, "The building of community, however, will require more than programming; it will require an institutional commitment [e.g., funding and resources] to the principles of multiculturalism and diversity" (p. 5). Because of the variance in organizational structure of institutions, the responsibility and funding for programming for diverse student populations will differ. Many times, offices are not allocated proper resources to host regional, national, or internationally recognized speakers or major cultural events. More often than not, cultural centers have budgets that cannot support, nor sustain, an active programming calendar. As a result, these offices can only afford to do one or two smaller programs, which may cause cultural centers, units, and departments programming to be seen as successful or impactful.

While the amount of money, time, and resources allocated to programming for students from underrepresented groups can be seen as a measure of an institution's commitment to diversity, programming initiatives are often among the first to be eliminated. Whether in student affairs or academic affairs units, providing sustainable, permanent funding for programming initiatives is a necessity and requires a commitment from administration to

NEW DIRECTIONS FOR STUDENT SERVICES • DOI: 10.1002/ss

ensure funding. Activity fee dollars acquired from student fees provide great resources and opportunities for programming. Programming boards housed in a college union may have greater access to these funds. Activity fee dollars and institutional monies should be used to provide programming that is educational, engaging, challenging, and entertaining for institutions with programming boards. Money should be allocated in a way that is consistent with the mission and vision of the institution, which makes it more critical that a college union's mission not only supports the larger university's but also includes diversity and inclusion. Programming committees that focus on diversity programming should not be shortchanged.

Staffing. College unions present a unique opportunity to bring together students, faculty, and staff from a variety of backgrounds, beliefs, orientations, and experiences. Preisinger and Wilson (1992) posited that a diverse staff may provide students with positive role models whose backgrounds and experiences are like the students they serve, and will also provide opportunity for colleagues to teach and learn from one another. Leading these efforts to bring together the campus community should be professionals who understand the value of diversity and are willing and able to work with diverse populations. It is imperative for institutions to hire professionals who are interculturally proficient, meaning they possess "the ability to successfully communicate, understand, and interact among persons with differing assumptions that exist because of ethnic or cultural orientations" (ACUI [Intercultural Proficiency], n.d., para. 1). Because the demographics of the student population are changing at a fast pace, staff members will need to keep abreast of these changes and how they can respond to the needs and wants of our students.

Professionals working in college unions have developed strategies to diversify the demographics of the organization. Through the professional association, ACUI, college union professionals have established mentoring programs for promising undergraduates and union professional staff from underrepresented populations, establishing practicum programs for graduate students at diverse institutional environments, and state that "assess[ing] and strengthen[ing] the Association's commitment to and vision for a multicultural organization" (ACUI [Strategic plan 2006–2010], n.d., p. 2) is crucial to professional development in college unions. These action items suggest that college union staff cannot just hope for diverse, culturally competent professionals to work in the field; rather, administrators must be proactive in cultivating and continuously mentoring professionals from the undergraduate level to seasoned professionals working in college unions. Howard-Hamilton (2000) explained that culturally competent professionals should understand and be comfortable with their own multiple identities; suspend judgment; develop realistic goals and objectives; check assumptions and biases; and develop a climate for open dialogue, reflection and challenge, and support around issues of diversity. Organizations where professional staff within college unions reflect similar salient identities to the student with whom they wish to interact have been found to positively influence the advancement of the tenets associated with creating a multicultural organization which were originally defined by LeNorman Strong.

Conclusion

Serving today's increasingly diverse student populations in college unions requires professionals to recognize the demographic trends of student populations and the emerging populations with unique cultural values and needs. It requires intentionality in building and maintaining spaces of inclusion for students, faculty, staff, and community members so that they may connect with each other and celebrate their differences. Professionals within college unions must also clearly articulate the values of embracing diversity in word (mission statements) and deed (programming, allocation of funds and resources, and developing a diverse profession).

References

Association of College Unions International (ACUI). (n.d.). *Intercultural proficiency*. Retrieved from http://www.acui.org/content.aspx?menu_id=30&id=10208

Association of College Unions International (ACUI). (n.d.). *Strategic plan 2006–2010*. Retrieved from http://www.acui.org/uploadedFiles/About_ACUI/FINAL-Strategic %20Plan.pdf

Association of College Unions International (ACUI). (2008). *ACUI's multicultural awareness: A statement of commitment to and vision for a multicultural organization*. Retrieved from http://www.acui.org/content.aspx?menu_id=30&id=656

Astin, A. W. (1999). Student involvement: A developmental theory for higher education. *Journal of College Student Development, 40*(5), 518–529.

Banning, J. H., & Bartels, S. (1997). A taxonomy: Campus physical artifacts as communicators of campus multiculturalism. *NASPA Journal, 35*(1), 29–37.

Bourassa, D. M., & Kruger, K. (2002). The national dialogue on academic and student affairs collaboration. In A. Kezar, D. J. Hirsch, & C. Burack (Eds.), *New Directions for Student Services: No. 116. Understanding the role of academic and student affairs collaboration in creating a successful learning environment* (pp. 9–38). San Francisco, CA: Jossey-Bass.

Campus Pride. (n.d.). *Mission, vision & values*. Retrieved from http://www.campuspride .org/about/mission/

Campus Pride Index. (n.d.). *About index*. Retrieved from http://www.campusprideindex .org/about/default.aspx

César Chávez Student Center at San Francisco State University. (n.d.). *About us*. Retrieved from http://www.sfsustudentcenter.com/about

Hamrick, F. A., Rumann, C. B., & Associates. (2012). *Called to serve: A handbook on student veterans and higher education*. San Francisco, CA: Jossey-Bass.

Harper, S. R., & Quaye, S. J. (Eds.). (2009). *Student engagement in higher education: Theoretical perspectives and practical approaches for diverse populations*. New York, NY: Routledge.

Hawley, C. (2012, February 18). *NYPD monitored Muslim students all over northeast*. Retrieved from http://www.ap.org/Content/AP-In-The-News/2012/NYPD-monitored -Muslim-students-all-over-Northeast

Higher Education Research Institute. (n.d.). *The spiritual life of college students: A national study of college students' search for meaning and purpose.* Retrieved from http://spirituality.ucla.edu/docs/reports/Spiritual_Life_College_Students_Full _Report.pdf

Howard-Hamilton, M. (2000). Programming for multicultural competencies. In D. Lid-dell & J. Lund (Eds.), *New Directions for Student Services: No. 90. Programming approaches that make a difference* (pp. 67–78). San Francisco, CA: Jossey-Bass.

Institute of International Education. (2013). *Open doors 2012 fast facts.* Retrieved from http://www.iie.org/~/media/Files/Corporate/Open-Doors/Fast-Facts/Fast%20Facts %202012-final.pdf

Kuh, G. D. (2003). What we're learning about student engagement from NSSE. *Change, 35*(2), 24–32.

Kuh, G. D., Kinzie, J., Schuh, J. H., Whitt, E. J., & Associates. (2005). *Student success in college: Creating conditions that matter.* San Francisco, CA: Jossey-Bass.

Mallinckrodt, B., & Sedlacek, W. E. (1985). *Attitudes and preferences of members of the campus community toward the Adele H. Stamp Union (Counseling Center Research Report No. 9-85).* College Park, MD: University of Maryland.

Mallinckrodt, B., & Sedlacek, W. E. (2009). Student retention and the use of campus facility by race. *NASPA Journal, 46*(4), 566–572.

Milani, T. E., Eakin, J. T., & Brattain, W. E. (1992). The role of the college union and the future. In T. E. Milani & J. W. Johnston (Eds.), *New Directions for Student Services: No. 58. The college union in the year 2000* (pp. 3–10). San Francisco, CA: Jossey-Bass.

Milani, T. E., & Johnston, J. W. (Eds.). (1992). *New Directions for Student Services: No. 58. The college union in the year 2000.* San Francisco, CA: Jossey-Bass.

National Center for Education Statistics (NCES). (2011). *Projections of education statistics to 2020.* Retrieved from http://nces.ed.gov/programs/projections /projections2020/tables/table_29.asp?referrer=list

Portland Community College. (n.d.). *Multicultural centers.* Retrieved from http://www .pcc.edu/resources/culture/

Preisinger, G. J., & Wilson, B. (1992). Preparing the college union and student activities for the year 2000. In T. E. Milani & J. W. Johnston (Eds.), *New Directions for Student Services: No. 58. The college union in the year 2000* (pp. 61–73). San Francisco, CA: Jossey-Bass.

Rullman, L., & van den Kieboom, J. (2012). *Physical place on campus: A report on the summit on building community.* Washington, DC: Association of College Unions International.

Santiago, D., & Callan, P. (2010). *Ensuring America's future: Benchmarking Latino college completion to meet national goals: 2010–2020.* Washington, DC: Excelencia in Education.

Schlossberg, N. K. (1989). Marginality and mattering: Key issues in building community. In D. C. Roberts (Ed.), *New Directions for Student Services: No. 48. Designing campus activities to foster a sense of community* (pp. 5–15). San Francisco, CA: Jossey-Bass.

Strange, C. C., & Banning, J. H. (2001). *Educating by design: Creating campus learning environments that work.* San Francisco, CA: Jossey-Bass.

Strong, L. J. (1986). *Race relations for personal and organizational effectiveness* (Unpublished manuscript).

Sutton, M. (2006). Best practices for college unions and student activities: Multicultural and diversity programming. *The Bulletin, 74*(6). Retrieved from http://www.acui.org/publications/bulletin/article.aspx?issue=304&id=1844

Tinto, V. (1993). *Leaving college: Rethinking the causes and cures of student attrition* (2nd ed.). Chicago, IL: University of Chicago Press.

Torres, V., Howard-Hamilton, M. F., & Cooper, D. (2003). *Identity development of diverse populations: Implications for teaching and administration in higher education.* San Francisco, CA: Jossey-Bass.
University of Houston, Division of Student Affairs. (n.d.). *Strategic plan, 2013.* Retrieved from http://www.uh.edu/dsa/about_student_affairs/strategic_plan.html
University of Vermont. (n.d.). *Discover our values & history.* Retrieved from http://www.uvm.edu/~davis/?Page=discover.php&SM=menu_history.html
Webster, D. W., & Sedlacek, W. E. (1982). The differential impact of a university student union on campus subgroups. *NASPA Journal, 19*(2), 48–51.
Whitt, E. J., Nesheim, B. E., Guentzel, M. J., & Kellogg, A. H. (2008). Principles of good practice for academic and student affairs partnership programs. *Journal of College Student Development, 49*(3), 235–249.

WILLIE L. BANKS, JR., *is the associate dean of students at Cleveland State University.*

DEBRA L. HAMMOND *is the executive director of the University Student Union at California State University Northridge, one of the most culturally diverse institutions in the country.*

EBELIA HERNANDEZ *is an assistant professor at Rutgers, The State University of New Jersey, where she teaches in the College Student Affairs program.*

NEW DIRECTIONS FOR STUDENT SERVICES • DOI: 10.1002/ss

3

This chapter explores the role that college unions play in fostering meaningful engagement of students in their college experiences.

Student Engagement and College Unions

Thomas Lane, Brett Perozzi

Professionals working in college unions can help create campus environments that foster learning and build community, yet there is limited research focused on how college unions influence student engagement and contribute to student outcomes (NASPA, 2010). Student engagement can be defined as the amount of time and effort put forth by students toward activities linked to student success outcomes, and how institutions allocate their resources, provide services, and organize learning opportunities, so students are encouraged to participate and benefit from such educationally purposeful activities (Kuh, 2003, 2009). Student engagement is positively associated with such student learning gains as grades and critical thinking (Carini, Kuh, & Klein, 2006). Given Kuh's definition, and the importance placed on student engagement within higher education (Hu, 2011), critical questions for professionals working in college unions include what is the impact of college unions on student learning and how do college unions increase student engagement and assess the student learning opportunities offered through its programs, services, and facilities?

The extent to which students are involved in meaningful educational experiences has been shown to have outcomes related to student success (Kinzie & Kuh, 2004; Kuh, 2003). Student success is the broad goal for colleges and universities and can generally be defined to include such attributes as persistence (Hu, 2011), satisfaction, and graduation (Kuh, Kinzie, Schuh, Whitt, & Associates, 2005). Professionals working in college unions contribute to student success through positive, meaningful engagement of students in the cocurriculum by providing leadership programs, student employment opportunities, college union governance, student organization leadership positions, community volunteering experiences, and others. The cocurriculum directly complements the academic curriculum by providing degree-appropriate and career-related experiences for students and learning opportunities that are intentionally focused on outcomes mirroring those promoted for general education, for example, interpersonal communication and intercultural understanding (Association of American Colleges and Universities, 2013).

NEW DIRECTIONS FOR STUDENT SERVICES, no. 145, Spring 2014 © 2014 Wiley Periodicals, Inc.
Published online in Wiley Online Library (wileyonlinelibrary.com) • DOI: 10.1002/ss.20077

An increased focus defining what students learn via college unions is exemplified in the most recent college union standard of the Council for the Advancement of Standards (CAS, 2012). The updated standards call for college union professionals to identify appropriate learning outcomes that address such constructs as cognitive complexity and humanitarianism and civic engagement, while providing evidence that these outcomes have been influenced by involvement in a college union. In addition to using the CAS college union standard as a self-assessment tool, professionals in college unions should be knowledgeable regarding the learning outcomes expressed by the institution overall, general education outcomes, and be able to demonstrate how a college union's student outcomes align with those. Through such congruence, college union professionals can better define the union's role with the campus community and reinforce what students learn in the classroom.

Cocurricular Student Learning in College Unions

In addition to college unions' role in building community and bringing campus members together, the CAS (2012) standard for college unions includes student learning as an integral part of the union's mission. Through intentionally planned programs, services, and activities, college unions can serve as an effective bridge for connecting out-of-class experiences or cocurricular learning with classroom learning. This facilitative role can be traced back to the historical inception of college unions as a debate forum for developing communication and problem-solving competencies among Oxford and Cambridge students (Butts, 1971). More recently, significant attention has been focused on the articulation and assessment of student learning outcomes intended to demonstrate what students are learning as a result of their participation in programs or activities that occur outside of the classroom (Bresciani, Gardner, & Hickmott, 2009).

The cocurriculum in college unions mirrors many institutions' general education curriculum and learning outcomes. Generally, faculty members want students to master course content and to learn to become excellent communicators and critical thinkers. College union staff must work closely with faculty to ensure that out-of-class experiences match what students are learning and doing in the classroom. This necessitates interaction among faculty and professionals in college unions and ideally leads to synergy and clarity for students. Programs can be developed that encourage faculty–student interaction by reaching out to faculty to seek and discuss ideas. Students' involvement with faculty outside of the classroom and discussions around career aspirations are well known to be beneficial for students (Kuh, 2003; Kuh et al., 2005). One example of a college union program designed to foster this interaction is a buy one coffee/drink and get one free when a faculty member and a student are meeting together.

The common student affairs philosophy of developing the whole student (American Council on Education, 1949) can be refined for college unions through the use of complementary learning outcomes. For example, CAS (2012) standards for college unions offer six learning domains for use by college union professionals. The domains allow flexibility to adapt to particular institutional characteristics. The six learning domains are: (a) knowledge acquisition, integration, construction, and application; (b) cognitive complexity; (c) intrapersonal development; (d) interpersonal development; (e) humanitarianism and civic engagement; and (f) practical competence. A 2010 NASPA-led survey found that participation in college union programs taught students how to balance their social activities with academic requirements, improved their appreciation for the fine and performing arts, and improved their communication skills (NASPA, 2010).

California State University-Northridge (CSUN) is a successful example where intentionality regarding student learning outcomes is occurring within college unions. The CSUN Student Affairs division established learning outcomes for programs and services for each department. Specifically mentioned in planning documents is the expectation that outcomes will complement those found in general education and outcomes desired for CSUN undergraduates. The division identified "common learning themes" and "common learning outcomes" to guide departmental outcome development. An example of a CSUN common learning theme is "Achieving Capacity for Mutually Supportive Relationships" along with the associated common learning outcome that "[t]he student will use effective interpersonal communication skills" (California State University Northridge, 2009, p. 2). From this common theme and outcome, the CSUN college union articulated a measurable strategy requiring student employees working in college unions to participate in at least one interpersonal communications skills training session and be able to demonstrate these skills in their work environment.

From this strategy, college union professionals developed the assessable learning outcome of increasing the number of students who self-reported a proficiency at effective interpersonal communication skills as a result of participating in the training sessions and work experiences offered. Within the college union's assessment plan, the methodology for measuring learning was identified and results were shared, along with program improvement actions taken by staff as a result of data gathered. The type of intentionality demonstrated by CSUN regarding student learning within the college union reflects the commitment necessary to align with the broader institutional goals of engagement and student success.

How College Unions Foster Engagement

College unions engage students through a variety of opportunities and collaborations and act as the community center for the campus while providing a forum for bringing individuals together (NASPA, 2010). Leadership roles, meaningful work, and volunteer service are some of the ways in which college unions embrace student involvement in the campus community. Whether a student is producing major events, entering a poetry contest, serving as a club leader, or working as a food service worker, the range of opportunities is vast.

College unions are one of the few entities in higher education that can be a set of programs that embody institutional ideals (Butts, 1971) and, in many cases, also a physical structure (Perozzi & O'Brien, 2009). Because college unions' physical spaces typically are highly desired and enjoyed by a large cross section of a campus community, the planning and execution of physical spaces in the union can impact the culture of the college or university. Through this unique structure or conceptualization, college unions offer a variety of leadership and engagement opportunities for students. Given the complexity and diversity found among college union organizations, efforts to increase engagement can look different depending upon a college union's structure, mission, student employment opportunities, staff involvement, and other institutional factors.

Leadership and Civic Engagement Opportunities.   College unions provide a range of programming that can be student-produced or staff-led. The programs reach many people and their planning and execution afford plentiful opportunities for the engagement of students, faculty, and staff. These programs provide opportunities for college unions and student leaders to facilitate academic, social, and cultural events for the campus community that can support student learning outcomes.

Noted civic scholar Tom Ehrlich defined civic engagement as making "a difference in the civic life of our communities and developing the combination of knowledge, skills, value, and motivation to make that difference" (Ehrlich, 2000, p. vi). Professionals working in college unions may advise and work closely with elected and selected student government officers and programming board leaders. These high-profile student positions provide a platform, or a learning laboratory, for practicing skills critical for current and future success. Similar learning can be achieved through participating in service-related programs, such as volunteer involvement, service-learning activities, and community engagement and outreach. College union staff can facilitate and model the critical role of citizenship and civic engagement.

Employers seek students who have filled leadership roles, such as the ones that college unions provide, because they demonstrate evidence of key knowledge and workplace skills as college graduates (Budryk, 2013). These leadership experiences can be powerful, and in many cases the learning outcomes are documented, measured, and translated into cocurricular transcripts that can be used in tandem with academic transcripts. Cocurricular transcripts have been used as a method for quantifying learning, skills, and experience gained by students outside of the traditional classroom (Gutowski, 2006). Research indicates that undergraduate students' involvement in cocurricular activities leads to greater initial earning power in the labor market upon graduation (Hu & Wolniak, 2010) and personal development of critical thinking and relational skills (Kuh, 1995).

Employment. On many campuses, the college union is one of the largest employers of student workers. While research is mixed on the impacts of employment during college (Lang, 2012), results generally imply that students who work moderate hours on campus have greater educational success (variously defined and measured) than students who work off campus or who do not work (Perozzi, 2009). These structured roles can be transformational experiences for students, especially when designed intentionally, with the students' learning in mind. Students can be an integral aspect of the functioning and decision making of the organization. Students trained to act on behalf of administrative staff, such as college union building managers responsible for monitoring the college union's safety and service during evenings, weekends, and holidays, are regularly confronted with opportunities to learn and practice problem solving and display leadership skills (NASPA, 2010). Students working in areas such as room setups and custodial can learn valuable skills about teamwork and communication, and many career-focused opportunities exist with positions in marketing, food and beverage, web design, and so forth. Because international students cannot work off campus, college unions offer a plethora of employment opportunities for this population of students. Getting students engaged in the campus community via employment opportunities connects them to resources, peer groups, and events that expose them to multiple perspectives and opinions.

Intentional development and transparent discussion with students about learning outcomes in the employment setting can be essential for student success (Perozzi, Kappes, & Santucci, 2009). Students who are employed by a college union are more involved with college union programs and activities than students who are not employed in a union (NASPA, 2010). When students are working on campus they are more likely to come in contact with faculty and staff members and spend time with their peers engaging in both academic and social realms. Framing these interactions and relationships with intentional outcomes can assist students with the development of key skills and abilities that can ultimately make them more marketable in the work force.

Roles of Staff. Professionals working in college unions play a critical role in connecting students to their campus experience and helping them sort through myriad options, choices, and decisions. Reaching out to students, fostering appropriate and meaningful relationships with them (a healthy student–staff partnership), and helping students and faculty connect are critical elements of college union programs and services.

Kinzie and Kuh (2004) found that effective institutions have strong senior leadership, who support staff broadly, and have a deep sense of purpose in their approach to student success. These leaders support a wide distribution of staff who are empowered to foster student engagement in high impact programs and practices. This has implications regarding the knowledge base and competencies required for college union directors and those they report to, as well as other college union staff. In addition to understanding human development theories, college union professionals need to have an appropriate student engagement framework that guides their work with students. Pomerantz (2006) discussed that over time the student affairs paradigm has moved from student services, to student development, to student learning, and now is a time for student engagement. Being knowledgeable about current trends and research is critical for all levels of staffing within college unions to support successful student engagement. However, this requires a commitment to continuing professional development especially when senior administrators who oversee college unions do not have a student affairs or college union background.

Understanding the demographics and unique characteristics of an institution's student body can help college union professionals identify strategies for programs and services that facilitate connections for as many students as possible. For example, the National Survey of Student Engagement (NSSE) showed that some students are generally more engaged than others: women, full-time students, students living on campus, international students, and those with diversity experiences (Kuh, 2003). Knowing this information can help college union professionals identify strategies for programs and services that facilitate connections for as many students as possible and develop approaches that foster engagement in purposeful activities. Working across areas and departments within the division of student affairs can also bring about synergy, resource savings, and collaboration among students and student groups. Additionally, as Banks, Hammond, and Hernandez discuss in Chapter 2, collaborations can assist with programming for diversity and multiple identities.

Relationships among students and professionals in college unions are vital, difficult, and everchanging. While research exists on the way students learn and develop and how practitioners can use these concepts (Evans, Forney, Guido, & Patton, 2009), it remains difficult to translate learning theory into practice. Students who are in volunteer or leadership positions within college unions may be advised by professionals in college unions in nonemployment relationships and not supervised, as a student employee would be. Supervision in employment relationships is well established, but advising students is much less defined. McCluskey-Titus (2004) advocated that staff conceptualize their roles more as mentors than advisors when working directly with student volunteers. This student–staff relationship is not always well understood across an institution and experiences can be rewarding while challenging (Dunkel & Schuh, 1997). Advising students in volunteer roles is done through carefully cultivated relationships that engender trust and respect. These nuanced interpersonal connections are often the domain of young, new professionals, who are tasked with working directly with students to help them succeed in college and develop solid life skills.

Physical and Design Elements.   As Rullman and Harrington discuss in Chapter 4, the physical aspects of college unions can have a significant impact on the ability of students to fully engage in their college experience. From 18-year-old students to students working full-time with families, the physical nature and design of college unions create spaces that facilitate or inhibit learning and meaningful connections (Knell & Latta, 2006). Making sure that physical space within college unions is inviting and safe for all members of the campus community is critical in setting the stage for deep engagement of students.

The physical structure of college unions is often its defining element. Most professionals in college unions favor that the organization be defined as a set of programs and ideas that work together to create community and engagement for the college or university (Butts, 1971). While acknowledging that a college union is more than its physical characteristics, this aspect of what a union provides to the campus community can be powerful. Design and implementation of diverse, unique, energetic, and soothing spaces provide for a dynamic element in the lives of college students and the campus community. College unions and other campus spaces can affect students' decisions about where to go to college and, therefore, can influence institutional recruitment strategies (Kirshstein & Kadamus, 2012; NASPA, 2010). Knowledge of design and impact of spaces on community drives renovation and construction processes that have lasting effects on generations of students. As discussed more in Chapter 4, intentional design related to general concepts, such as location, size, common space, and amenities, as well as attention to specific detail related to service adjacencies, opacity of meeting and conference rooms, and furniture choices can impact the way in which students come together and ultimately learn in their academic environment (Orlando, 2000). Physical artifacts embody and communicate cultural messages to students, and should be carefully considered in college union spaces (Banning & Bartels, 1997).

Measuring Student Engagement

It takes students, faculty, and staff working together to set direction and support student success efforts (Kinzie & Kuh, 2004). Success should be defined collaboratively and measures of student engagement can be agreed upon across the institution including the college union. As such, college union professionals should "assess relevant and desirable student learning and development" and "provide evidence of impact on outcomes" (CAS, 2012, p. 5). Effectively demonstrating the student learning occurring within the college union and connecting that learning to broader institutional goals such as those embedded within general education better defines the college union's connection to, and alignment with, the overall mission of the educational institution (Bresciani et al., 2009). To be successful, college union professionals must be competent in articulating program learning goals aligned with institutional and divisional priorities, identifying measurable learning outcomes assessing what learning has occurred using a variety of methods, succinctly reporting assessment data, and using data gathered to continually improve programs and activities offered.

One method for understanding general student engagement at a college or university is through the use of the National Survey of Student Engagement (NSSE). While NSSE will not provide specific information about college union engagement efforts, staff can track their efforts over time in relation to their institution's engagement scores on NSSE. Texas A&M Corpus Christi provides one example of how NSSE data can be useful to a college union. The university provided longitudinal analysis of NSSE items relevant to college unions, such as results on the time students spend on cocurricular activities and the extent to which students perceive an emphasis on attending campus events (NSSE, 2012).

Most professionals working in college unions know such information as how many people visit the facility each day, what they do while there, and to some extent who those individuals are. Finding out if those individuals are satisfied with the programs and services offered can also help college unions change and grow. Professionals in college unions would be wise to monitor institutional student success indicators, such as retention, persistence, and graduation rates to better understand how union engagement efforts can help move forward the college or university's enrollment management plan. Demonstrating, for instance, that students who are engaged with college union leadership or employment roles have better grades, and/or are retained at higher levels can help position college unions to garner funding and add or expand programs and services. Measuring the extent to which students learn the outcomes associated with engagement efforts should be the ultimate goal of college unions. The ability to articulate what students have learned as a direct result of college union programs and services can be powerful data for accreditation, resource requests, and other assessment efforts.

It is the student's responsibility to acquire skills and gain knowledge, and the institution's and the college union's responsibility to provide the environment in which students can learn and develop (Axelson & Flick, 2010). A focus on learning outcomes is a compelling way to demonstrate students are benefiting from their involvement with college unions. Defined learning outcomes can be measured directly by reframing evaluations from satisfaction-related or generally measuring value derived from a program, to asking students to name or list specific skills or knowledge they learned during an activity. Another way to help isolate program impact is to use a control group of students with similar characteristics to the one being assessed. For example, when evaluating student employees, it is possible to reflect against a population of students who do not work.

A number of other methods are available for college union staff to measure learning. Focus groups using set or standardized questions that relate directly to pre-defined learning outcomes can be a relatively simple way to gain insight into student learning (Krueger & Casey, 2009). While potentially time consuming, focus groups will provide rich data about skill and knowledge development. Reflection papers, journals, rubrics, and survey tools can also assist staff in measuring and reporting learning gains of students (Mason & Meyer, 2012).

Conclusion

A central element of college union work is designing and maintaining environments that foster student engagement in programs and activities that are positively associated with satisfaction, persistence, and learning. It is important that college union professionals understand a college union's roles on a college campus and can demonstrate a commitment to student learning and engagement throughout all aspects of the organization, so the college union can be well positioned for assisting students in meaningfully connecting with faculty, staff, and one another. A college union's programs, services, and facilities help provide a learning laboratory for students to exercise their cognitive and affective muscles in a safe, supportive, yet challenging environment.

Critical for success is understanding how the curricular and the cocurricular elements of college union programs and initiatives fit together and how college unions can meaningfully support student engagement and the overall institutional learning goals through its offerings. A key organizing element for college unions is to ensure that all members of a college union's staff are knowledgeable about the importance of student engagement in supporting the institution's academic endeavors. It is critical for organizational success to gather data that demonstrates how programs and services offered through a college union affect students and to what extent students are learning via these activities. Using such data to drive resource allocation decisions (such as fiscal, personnel, and space) helps ensure organizational alignment with the institution's academic mission, resulting in the college union serving a powerful force in furthering student engagement and enhancing institutional life.

References

American Council on Education. (1949). *The student personnel point of view* Washington, DC: Author.

Association of American Colleges and Universities. (2013, February 18). *Global learning VALUE rubric*. Paper presented at the Association of International Education Administrators Conference, New Orleans, LA.

Axelson, R. D., & Flick, A. (2010). Defining student engagement. *Change: The Magazine of Higher Learning, 43*(1), 38–43.

Banning, J. H., & Bartels, S. (1997). A taxonomy: Campus physical artifacts as communicators of campus multiculturalism. *NASPA Journal, 35*(1), 29–38.

Bresciani, M. J., Gardner, M. M., & Hickmott, J. (2009). *Demonstrating student success: A practical guide to outcomes-based assessment of learning and development in student affairs*. Sterling, VA: Stylus.

Budryk, Z. (2013, April 10). Survey finds that business executives aren't focused on the majors of those they hire. *Inside Higher Ed.* Retrieved from http://www.insidehighered.com/news/2013/04/10/survey-finds-business-executives-arent-focused-majors-those-they-hire

Butts, P. (1971). *The college union idea.* Stanford, CA: Association of College Unions International.

California State University Northridge. (2009). *University student union learning outcomes.* Retrieved from http://www.csun.edu/sites/default/files/student_affairs_priorities_clts_outcomes.pdf

Carini, R., Kuh, G. D., & Klein, S. P. (2006). Student engagement and student learning: Testing the linkages. *Research in Higher Education, 47*(1), 1–32.

Council for the Advancement of Standards in Higher Education (CAS). (2012). *CAS professional standards for higher education* (8th ed.). Washington, DC: Author.

Dunkel, N. W., & Schuh, J. H. (1997). *Advising student groups and organizations.* San Francisco, CA: Jossey-Bass.

Ehrlich, T. (2000). *Civic responsibility and higher education.* Phoenix, AZ: Oryx Press.

Evans, N., Forney, D., Guido, F., & Patton, L. (2009). *Student development in college: Theory, research, and practice.* San Francisco, CA: Jossey-Bass.

Gutowski, J. (2006). Cocurricular transcripts: Documenting holistic higher education. *ACUI The Bulletin, 74*(5). Retrieved from https://www.acui.org/publications/bulletin/article.aspx?issue=306&id=1900

Hu, S. (2011). Reconsidering the relationship between student engagement and persistence in college. *Innovative Higher Education, 36*(2), 97–106.

Hu, S., & Wolniak, G. (2010). Initial evidence on the influence of college student engagement on early career earnings. *Research in Higher Education, 51*(8), 750–766.

Kinzie, J., & Kuh, G. D. (2004). Going DEEP: Learning from campuses that share responsibility for student success. *About Campus, 9*(5), 2–8.

Kirshstein, R., & Kadamus, J. (2012). *Climbing walls and climbing tuitions.* The Delta Cost Project. Washington, DC: AIR.

Knell, P., & Latta, S. (2006). *College union dynamic: Flexible solutions for successful facilities.* Bloomington, IN: ACUI.

Krueger, R. A., & Casey, M. A. (2009). *Focus groups: A practical guide for applied research.* Thousand Oaks, CA: Sage.

Kuh, G. D. (1995). The other curriculum: Out-of-class experiences associated with student learning and personal development. *Journal of Higher Education, 66*(2), 123–155.

Kuh, G. D. (2003). What we're learning about student engagement from NSSE. *Change: The Magazine of Higher Learning, 35*(2), 24–32.

Kuh, G. D. (2009). What student affairs professionals need to know about student engagement. *Journal of College Student Development, 50*(6), 683–699.

Kuh, G. D., Kinzie, J., Schuh, J., Whitt, E., & Associates. (2005). *Student success in college: Creating conditions that matter.* San Francisco, CA: Jossey-Bass.

Lang, K. B. (2012). The similarities and differences between working and non-working students at a mid-sized American public university. *College Student Journal, 46*(2), 243–255.

Mason, T. A., & Meyer, S. W. (2012). Using outcomes and rubrics in student affairs. In M. Culp & G. Dungy (Eds.), *Building a culture of evidence in student affairs* (pp. 61–87). Washington, DC: NASPA.

McCluskey-Titus, P. (2004, January 20). Student organization adviser as mentor: A different paradigm? *NetResults*. Washington, DC: NASPA.

NASPA. (2010). *Senior student affairs officer: 2010 executive report.* Washington, DC: NASPA.

National Survey of Student Engagement (NSSE). (2012). *Moving from data to action: Lessons from the field—Volume 2.* Bloomington: Indiana University Center for Postsecondary Research.

Orlando, C. E. (2000). The collegium: Community as gathering place. In B. Jacoby (Ed.), *New Directions for Higher Education: No. 109. Involving commuter students in learning* (pp. 33–41). San Francisco, CA: Jossey-Bass.

Perozzi, B. (Ed.). (2009). *Enhancing student learning through college employment.* Bloomington, IN: ACUI.

Perozzi, B., Kappes, J., & Santucci, D. (2009). Learning outcomes and student employment programs. In B. Perozzi (Ed.), *Enhancing student learning through college employment* (pp. 67–84). Bloomington, IN: ACUI.

Perozzi, B., & O'Brien, A. (2009). College unions/university centres/student centres. In R. Ludeman, K. Osfield, E. Iglesias Hidalgo, D. Oste, & H. S. Wang (Eds.), *Student affairs and services in higher education: Global foundations, issues, and best practices* (2nd ed., pp. 94–96). Paris, France: UNESCO.

Pomerantz, N. K. (2006). Student engagement: A new paradigm for student affairs. *The College Student Affairs Journal, 25*(2), 176–185.

THOMAS LANE *is the assistant vice president for Student Life and director of the Plaster Student Union at Missouri State University and is an adjunct faculty for MSU's Higher Education and Student Affairs program.*

BRETT PEROZZI *is the associate vice president for Student Affairs at Weber State University and the chair of the International Advisory Board for NASPA-Student Affairs Administrators in Higher Education.*

This chapter examines the importance of college union facilities to create community and to enhance the role of college unions as the "living room of the campus."

College Unions, Learning, and Community Building

Loren J. Rullman, Kim D. Harrington

We never educate directly, but indirectly by means of the environment. Whether we permit chance environments to do the work, or whether we design environments for the purpose makes a great difference.

(Dewey, 1916, p. 22)

This is a time of profound change in higher education, as concerns about the rising cost of higher education collide with the reality that large sums of money are spent on campus facilities, resulting in political optics that are challenging to explain to the general public (Blumenstyk, 2012). This explanation may be most challenging when expenditures include nonacademic facilities, such as college unions. In 2011, almost $12 billion was spent on campus facilities with two thirds of it on new construction (Basu, 2011). The median price of a newly constructed college union facility was a sizable $21 million (Abramson, 2011).

As a consequence, it is important that college unions are aligned explicitly with the academic mission of the institutions they support. If they are not so aligned, the mission of college unions is jeopardized. When constructed and managed with intentionality, college unions can make lasting and fundamentally important contributions to student learning and students' college experiences. While college unions are much more than facilities, the value of their physical structures to students' educational experiences is considerable. By examining the influence of architecture and the physical campus on student behavior, professionals in college unions can create physical environments for learning and facilitate a sense of belonging for students.

NEW DIRECTIONS FOR STUDENT SERVICES, no. 145, Spring 2014 © 2014 Wiley Periodicals, Inc.
Published online in Wiley Online Library (wileyonlinelibrary.com) • DOI: 10.1002/ss.20078

Architectural Theory and College Unions

Before considering the impact of a college union's facility upon its users, it is important to consider more generally the influence of architecture itself on the environment. The impact of facilities upon how people feel, behave, and interact with each other has long been documented by contemporary authors (London, 2010; Tupper, Carson, Johnston, & Mangat, 2008) who continue to apply John Dewey's (1916) belief about the importance of space to identity development and learning. Lewin (1936) suggested with his formula of $B = f(P, E)$ that behavior can be understood as a function of the interaction between the person and the environment. More specifically, the literature offers three essential perspectives about the influence of architecture: conceptualized as architectural determinism, architectural probabilism, and architectural possibilism (Devlin, 2010).

The premise of the first perspective, architectural determinism, is that human behavior is largely predictable and caused almost mechanistically by the physical environment. This perspective suggests that the placement of furniture, walls, doors, and other artifacts will cause recurring and consistent responses by facility users. For example, based on the placement of these structures, people will exit a lounge in consistently predictable ways. The second perspective, architectural probabilism, suggests that behavior is not entirely predictable and that the probability of behavior responses can be enhanced with thoughtful facility design. For example, a student lounge that is well lit, nicely furnished, and easy to find may increase the likelihood of use. The third perspective, architectural possibilism, assumes a predetermined response is unlikely and that all physical features have an equal opportunity to affect the user experience. Devlin (2010) summarized these three perspectives simply as follows: "determinism suggests the design created the outcome; probabilism suggests the design makes a certain outcome more likely, and possibilism suggests the environment creates the opportunity for an outcome" (p. 119).

To those working in the college union field, these perspectives are helpful, but insufficient, to fully explain human behavior given the vast complexities of social and psychological differences found on most campuses. This is especially true given the diversity of people that, by definition and intention, inhabit college union environments (Alleman, Holly, & Costello, 2012; Banning & Cunard, 1996; Strange & Banning, 2001). Indeed, as Cuyjet, Howard-Hamilton, and Cooper (2011) reported, because of the inadequacy of architecture alone to explain what occurs inside a facility, "it becomes necessary to examine the impact of the environment in smaller, more focused, less general terms to observe how the same element of the environment can have different—sometimes minutely, sometimes drastically— effects on the inhabitants of the community" (p. 37). Cuyjet et al. explained that the degree of homogeneity within a population, and the characteristics of dominant populations relative to subpopulations, can affect the impact

NEW DIRECTIONS FOR STUDENT SERVICES • DOI: 10.1002/ss

of the human aggregate upon a particular environment. That is, the cultural conditioning that people bring to a campus affects the ways they experience the architecture of that campus. For example, the individualism of American culture may result in greater distance between lounge seating than is characteristic of other cultures, which are more comfortable with collective and social interaction. Or, a historically accurate display of the college union organization's White male founders may be deemed reverential by some, but insensitive by those with deep interest in issues of inclusion. In sum, the relationship between a space and its users is not solely a product of the architecture, yet the physical framework of a campus and the design of its facilities play a role in human experiences.

College Union Facilities' Impacts on Students

The physical campus as an entity conveys intended and unintended messages to students, employees, and visitors. The cleanliness and manicure of the campus, the condition of the facilities, the location of needed services, and the availability of open space all send messages or "non-verbal cues" about what the institutional values (Strange & Banning, 2001, p. 16). If, for example, an institution imagines itself as highly accessible, with low barriers to student success, and deeply focused on student support, then placement of its admissions, financial aid, advising, and child care services at the edge of campus rather than at its core, or in low quality or unkempt spaces, may convey incongruence between what it values and what it does. On the other hand, an institutional culture that believes learning is derived from frequent student engagement with peers, active and self-directed cocurricular involvement, and regular exposure to diverse perspectives may illustrate these values by locating its student organization offices, its collaborative spaces, and its multicultural programming along primary campus pathways and in highly visible locations. Since college union facilities often host offices and opportunities for student engagement and cocurricular involvement, their location and condition send nonverbal messages as Strange and Banning's (2001) research showed. Physical structures are the means by which the institution communicates nonverbally to its users about its values, vision, and capabilities.

Although no university with a physical campus can easily exist without formal instruction space, it is often "the informal territory of collegiate life between these important [academic] settings that can have the most impact" (Atkins & Oakland, 2008, "Useful applications," para. 1). Kuh, Schuh, and Whitt (1991) suggested that nonacademic spaces are important because "interaction among community members is fostered by the availability of indoor and outdoor spaces where people can come together without much effort. Institutions should consider whether their campuses have adequate places that encourage spontaneous, informal interactions among students" (p. 309). Student-focused spaces, like the Union Terrace at the University of Wisconsin, serve as emblems of the institution's core values, as literal and symbolic bridges between faculty and students, and as physical vehicles for teaching institutional traditions (Atkins & Oakland, 2008).

Increasingly, higher education leaders recognize the value of campus spaces that are flexible, can enhance collaboration, and provide greater access to technology (Beichner et al., 2007; Massis, 2010). Jamieson (2003), for example, asserted that universities "need spaces designed to generate interaction, collaboration, physical movement, and social engagement as primary elements of the student learning experience" (p. 121). Professionals in college unions purposefully engineer experiences for students to interact with others. As such, college union facilities designed for this purpose are well situated for the learning Jamieson (2003) described. Indeed, the physical campus is "both functional and symbolic" (Strange & Banning, 2001, p. 15), and the college union is uniquely important to both.

College union facilities influence community, learning, and engagement due to the social implications of space or what Strange and Banning (2001) referred to as proxemics. For example, the overt and covert messages sent by seating arrangements, cleanliness, signage, types of offices, and accessibility all influence human feelings, behavior, interaction, engagement, energy level, attitude, and even how much time individuals will spend in a facility. Spaces can signal feelings of control or emancipation, interaction or isolation, acceptance or rejection, community or invisibility (Tupper et al., 2008). In fact, one study found that behaviors of people can be more accurately understood by the settings they are in than from the individual characteristics of the inhabitants themselves (Kenney, Dumont, & Kenney, 2005). As noted previously, Cuyjet et al. (2011) discussed that physical artifacts can evoke nonverbal responses that can be negative or positive, and are either aligned or misaligned with institutional intention. Further, interpretation is always culturally understood or received within an individual's cultural context. For example, an architecturally imposing college union sends a signal to students about the importance of cocurricular life, or a women's center in the basement of a peripheral facility sends a message about the centrality of women's concerns. Moreover, when verbal (e.g., women's concerns are important) and nonverbal (e.g., a peripheral location for the women's center) messages are received, the nonverbal communication is typically more believable (Cuyjet et al., 2011; Strange & Banning, 2001).

Psychosocial and behavioral responses are positively influenced by a myriad of facility elements, including the existence of and ease of movement between spaces for prospect (visual access to other people) and refuge (feeling safe and protected); natural daylight and artifacts; sensory variability; occupant sense of agency or ownership; flexibility of space and furnishings; opportunities for spontaneous social encounters; moderate sound levels; presence of social equity and respect between people; food and other stimuli for ritual and relationship building; and purposeful mixing of offices, services, programs, and spaces that invite and retain the campus community (i.e., academic support, meeting and study spaces, student life programs, private and social lounges, essential student services, welcoming areas, student organization, and involvement spaces; Atkins & Oakland, 2008; Heerwagen, 2008; Rullman & van den Kieboom, 2012).

College Union Facilities as Places for Learning

The quality and quantity of student engagement in both the academic and cocurricular aspects of a college environment enhance learning and skill development (Pascarella & Terenzini, 2005). The literature is replete with evidence that a relationship exists between student learning and student involvement and that campus community including physical design has an impact on student learning, academic persistence, and student retention (Astin, 1993; Kuh, Cruce, Shoup, Kinzie, & Gonyea, 2008; Kuh et al., 1991; Palmer, Maramba, & Elon Dancy, 2011; Strange & Banning, 2001; Tinto, 1987; Tinto, Goodsell-Love, & Russo, 1993). Conditions that contribute to campus community include, for example, meaningful faculty–student interaction (NASPA, 2010; Zhao & Kuh, 2004), participation in educationally purposeful activities (Kinzie & Schuh, 2008; Palmer et al., 2011), student involvement in cocurricular and social aspects of college life (Cheng, 2004; Elkins, Forrester, & Noel-Elkins, 2011), and availability of quality services to support diverse student needs (Nasir & Al-Amin, 2006).

Bickford and Wright (2006) described the catalyzing role that community has upon learning and how community-based learning causes "members [to] interact in a meaningful way that deepens their understanding of each other and leads to learning" (p. 4.2). That is, interaction and dialogue with others causes reflection, introspection, values clarification, and a sense of self, with both private interests and concomitant responsibilities to others (London, 2010). Community created in college unions can help individuals apply what is learned in and beyond the classroom, while also experimenting with meaningful interaction and a deepening of understanding about self and others. College unions provide such opportunities through, for example, programming boards and student organizations that plan lectures, cultural activities, and social events in college unions to educate and challenge other students, while simultaneously offering powerful learning experiences for the students who comprise these boards and organizations (Joint Task Force on Student Learning, 1998).

Places are physical domains where interactions between individuals and groups generate social meaning (Marcouyeux & Fleury-Bahi, 2011). Since learning and community building are optimally social processes that develop meaning making, highlight memories, and create institutional stories (Broussard, 2009), it is critical that a college union's spaces provide intentional opportunities for meaningful interactions with peers, staff, and faculty, who are critical to quality learning experiences (Kuh, Kinzie, Schuh,

Whitt, & Associates, 2010). To that end, college unions are ideal physical environments for all members of the institutional family to be welcomed into meaningful interaction and relationship building, and for learning to be of the highest quality.

College Union Facilities as Places for Belonging

College unions can be places for individual students to feel part of a larger community of learners. If learning is social, and a sense of community is vital to the learning process, then students need to feel a part of the community to take full advantage of all possible learning experiences. As this volume describes elsewhere, college unions have a unique role to play in cultivating feelings of belonging and affinity to the institution and in serving individual student needs. As a result of participating in programs and activities housed in college unions, a majority of students feel a part of the campus community (NASPA, 2010). Schlossberg's (1989) marginality and mattering research explained that students who engage in the campus community experience a sense of mattering, that is they feel included and cared for by others in the community. On the other hand, students who do not feel like they matter to others experience marginality, which is characterized by feelings of isolation and exclusion. Students who feel marginalized are unlikely to participate fully in college life. Chronic feelings of marginality can harm a student's physical and psychological health, self-efficacy, and overall academic success and retention.

Because a college union, by definition, "honors each individual and values diversity" (Association of College Unions International, 1996, para. 5), the intention developed around the construction of a college union facility may contain services, support, programs, and offices designed to mitigate feelings of isolation and enhance feelings of belonging. In this way, a college union conveys that the institution is responsive to student needs and invites students into a community with others who care about them while offering myriad opportunities for learning and engagement (Strange & Banning, 2001).

Future Considerations

Although this chapter addressed primarily the importance of a college union facility to student learning, engagement, and the overall sense of community, college union professionals increasingly must be cognizant of many other issues and trends. These include, for example, sustainable construction and operations (Radoff, 2011); economic pressures and privatization of institutional services (Russell, 2010); safety management and emergency operations (NACUBO, 2009); and, as noted elsewhere, technological changes which affect operations and services found in college unions. Each of these topics is beyond the scope of this chapter, but are worthy of further exploration in their own right and serve as examples of the multifaceted role that a college union plays for institutions of higher education.

Conclusion

As a result of what is known about the influence of involvement and community on learning, about the importance of facility design on human behavior, and about the role of a college union in achieving the institution's objectives, it is imperative that college union facilities be designed and managed with intended outcomes in mind and with flexibility to be responsive over time. College union facilities do not have a uniform template. Individual college union facilities should take into account the campus' physical framework and the symbolism of its location in context of campus and local demographics. Furthermore, the nature and needs of the campus population, the appropriate mix of what is contained within its walls, and the understanding of proxemics should be considered in its design.

References

Abramson, P. (2011). *The 2011 college construction report.* Retrieved from http://www.peterli.com/cpm/pdfs/CollegeConstructionReport2011.pdf

Alleman, N., Holly, L. N., & Costello, C. A. (2012). Agency and influence: The organizational impact of a new school of education building. *Planning for Higher Education, 41*(2), 1–10.

Association of College Unions International. (1996). *Role of the college union.* Retrieved from http://www.acui.org/content.aspx?menu_id=30&id=296

Astin, A. (1993). *What matters in college?* San Francisco, CA: Jossey-Bass.

Atkins, J., & Oakland, D. (2008). College unions transform campus life at small regional institutions. *The Bulletin, 76*(3). Retrieved from http://www.acui.org/publications/bulletin/article.aspx?issue=700&id=6954

Banning, J., & Cunard, M. (1996). An ecological perspective of buildings and behavior: Implications for the renovation and construction of the college union. *College Services Administration, 19*(4), 38–41.

Basu, A. (2011). *Higher education construction spending: Peak, slump, recover?* Retrieved from http://www.constructionexec.com/Issues/June_2011/Economic_Outlook.aspx

Beichner, R., Saul, J., Abbott, D., Morse, J., Deardorff, D., Allain, R., ... Risely, J. (2007). *The Student Centered Activities for Large Enrollment Undergraduate Programs (SCALE-UP) Project.* Retrieved from http://www.per-central.org/items/detail.cfm?ID=4517

Bickford, D., & Wright, D. (2006). Community: The hidden context of learning. In D. G. Oblinger (Ed.), *Learning spaces.* Boulder, CO: EDUCAUSE. Retrieved from http://net.educause.edu/ir/library/pdf/PUB7102d.pdf

Blumenstyk, G. (2012). College officials welcome Obama's focus on higher-education costs, but raise some concerns. *The Chronicle of Higher Education.* Retrieved from http://chronicle.com/article/President-Puts-College-Costs/130503/

Broussard, E. (2009, May 1). The power of place on campus. *The Chronicle of Higher Education.* Retrieved from http://chronicle.com/article/The-Power-of-Place-on-Campus/3399

Cheng, D. (2004). Students' sense of campus community: What it means, and what to do about it. *NASPA Journal, 41*(2), 216–234.

Cuyjet, M., Howard-Hamilton, M., & Cooper, D. (2011). *Multiculturalism on campus: Theory, models, and practices for understanding diversity and creating inclusion*. Sterling, VA: Stylus.

Devlin, A. (2010). *What Americans build and why: Psychological perspectives*. Cambridge, MA: Cambridge University Press.

Dewey, J. (1916). *Democracy and education: An introduction to the philosophy of education*. New York, NY: Macmillian.

Elkins, D. J., Forrester, S. A., & Noel-Elkins, A. V. (2011). Students' perceived sense of campus community: The influence of out of class experiences. *College Student Journal, 45*(1), 105–121.

Heerwagen, J. (2008). *Psychosocial value of space*. Retrieved from http://www .wbdg.org/resources/psychspace_value.php

Jamieson, P. (2003). Designing more effective on campus teaching and learning spaces: A role for academic developers. *International Journal for Academic Development, 8*(1–2), 119–133.

Joint Task Force on Student Learning. (1998, June). *Powerful partnerships: A shared responsibility for learning*. Retrieved from http://www.nova.edu/cwis /saase/forms/powerful_partnerships.pdf

Kenney, D., Dumont, R., & Kenney, G. (2005). *Mission learning and community through campus design*. Westport, CT: Praeger Publishers.

Kinzie, J., & Schuh, J. H. (2008). DEEP (documenting effective educational practice) colleges and universities as communities. *NASPA Journal, 45*(3), 406–424.

Kuh, G. D., Cruce, T., Shoup, R., Kinzie, J., & Gonyea, R. (2008). Unmasking the effects of student engagement on first year college grades and persistence. *The Journal of Higher Education, 79*(5), 540–563.

Kuh, G. D., Kinzie, J., Schuh, J., Whitt, E., & Associates. (2010). *Student success in college*. San Francisco, CA: Jossey-Bass.

Kuh, G. D., Schuh, J., & Whitt, E. (1991). *Involving colleges. Successful approaches to fostering student learning and development outside the classroom*. San Francisco, CA: Jossey-Bass.

Lewin, K. (1936). *Principles of topological psychology*. New York, NY: McGraw-Hill.

London, D. (2010). *Building the great community: John Dewey and the public spaces of social democracy*. Retrieved from http://www.academia.edu /934760/Building_the_Great_Community_John_Dewey_and_ThePublic_Spaces_of _Social_Democracy

Marcouyeux, A., & Fleury-Bahi, G. (2011). Place-identity in a school setting: Effects of the place image. *Environment and Behavior, 43*(3), 344–362.

Massis, B. (2010). The academic library becomes the academic learning commons. *New Library World, 111*(3/4), 161–163.

Nasir, N., & Al-Amin, J. (2006). Creating identity safe spaces on college campuses for Muslim students. *Change, 38*(2), 22–27.

NASPA. (2010). *Senior student affairs officer: 2010 executive report*. Washington, DC: Author.

National Association of College and University Business Officers (NACUBO). (2009). *Results of the national campus safety and security project survey*. Retrieved from http://www.nacubo.org/Documents/Initiatives/CSSPSurveyResults.pdf

Palmer, R. T., Maramba, D. C., & Elon Dancy, T., II. (2011). A qualitative investigation of factors promoting the retention and persistence of students of color in stem. *The Journal of Negro Education, 80*(4), 491–504.

Pascarella, E., & Terenzini, P. (2005). *How college affects students: Vol. 2. A decade of research*. San Francisco, CA: Wiley.

Radoff, J. (2011). *Higher education—The vibrant epicenter of a sustainable future.* Retrieved from http://www.torkusa.com/Global/6_North_America/White%20Papers /Higher_Education_2011_White_Paper%2009-20-11%20FINAL%20_2_.pdf

Rullman, L., & van den Kieboom, J. (2012). Creating community: Designing spaces that make a difference. *Planning for Higher Education, 41*(1), 1–16.

Russell, A. (2010). *Outsourcing instruction: Issues for public colleges and universities.* American Association of State Colleges and Universities. Retrieved from http://www.aascu.org/policy/publications/policy-matters/2010/outsourcing.pdf

Schlossberg, N. K. (1989). Marginality and mattering: Key issues in building community. In D. C. Roberts (Ed.), *New Directions for Student Services: No. 48. Designing campus activities to foster a sense of community* (pp. 5–15). San Francisco, CA: Jossey-Bass.

Strange, C., & Banning, J. (2001). *Educating by design: Creating campus learning environments that work.* San Francisco, CA: Jossey-Bass.

Tinto, V. (1987, November). *Principles of effective retention.* Speech presented at the Maryland College Personnel Association Conference, Largo, MD.

Tinto, V., Goodsell-Love, A., & Russo, P. (1993). Building community. *Liberal Education, 79*(4), 16–21.

Tupper, J. A., Carson, T., Johnston, I., & Mangat, J. (2008). Building place: Students' negotiation of spaces and citizenship in schools. *Canadian Journal of Education, 31*(4), 1065–1092.

Zhao, C. M., & Kuh, G. D. (2004). Adding value: Learning communities and student engagement. *Research in Higher Education, 45*(2), 115–138.

Loren J. Rullman is an associate vice president for Student Affairs at the University of Michigan. He serves as ACUI representative on the Board of Directors of the Council for the Advancement of Standards in Higher Education.

Kim D. Harrington is the director of the Student Center at the Georgia Institute of Technology and currently serves as president-elect of the Association of College Unions International.

5

This chapter addresses ways college union professionals can establish partnerships and strategies for establishing fundraising and philanthropy initiatives within their organizations.

Fundraising and Philanthropy in College Unions

Danielle M. De Sawal, Daniel Maxwell

Funding building renovations, the addition of new facilities, and student programming within college unions can be challenging during the best of economic times. The reality of continued declines in government support and external pressure to reduce tuition expenses means that institutions are increasingly seeking private support to advance campus goals (Drezner, 2011). Public and private institutions have approached philanthropy differently over the past 100 years. Private institutions have been involved in institutional advancement since the early 1900s, while public institutions did not strategically approach philanthropy until the 1980s (Conley & Tempel, 2006). During the 2012 fiscal year, of the $31 billion in voluntary giving for U.S. college and university only 28% ($7.7 billion) were from alumni (Kaplan, 2013). The remaining gifts were given by nonalumni (18.8%), religious organizations (0.8%), corporations (16.9%), other organizations (9%), and foundations providing the largest percentage at 29.5% (Kaplan, 2013). Fundraising within student affairs has only recently grown as programs and services have been asked to do more with less as a result of institutional budget cuts. The college union is an area within student affairs that has the potential to establish successful fundraising initiatives (Schuh, 2011).

Limited literature exists about fundraising within student affairs, and even less has been written regarding fundraising for college unions. The role of fundraising in higher education has traditionally been associated with institutional foundations, which often exist as a separate nonprofit agency from the institution and the distribution of resources are frequently managed through the President's Office. Miller (2010) noted that fundraising may not be a natural task for student affairs administrators. However, the reality is that it will most likely be a necessity for individual functional areas within then student affairs profession to establish their own fundraising initiatives to have more control over bringing in additional funding

NEW DIRECTIONS FOR STUDENT SERVICES, no. 145, Spring 2014 © 2014 Wiley Periodicals, Inc.
Published online in Wiley Online Library (wileyonlinelibrary.com) • DOI: 10.1002/ss.20079

(Miller, 2010; Puma, 2013). Professionals working in college unions need to consider if they want to dedicate staff and resources to establishing a fundraising effort within their college union organization. The establishment of a fundraising effort is not a one-time event; rather a successful implementation is intentional and addresses both a long-term and a short-term focus (Dove, 2001) with alumni not being the sole source or focus for fundraising initiatives. This chapter will explore how to work with institutional foundations, cultivate donors, establish a student philanthropy program, and create a culture of giving for college unions.

Partnering With the University's Foundation

Establishing a strong connection across campus will be critical in ensuring a successful fundraising plan for the college union. Prior to developing a fundraising plan, professionals in college unions need to identify who their point of contact will be at their institution. Often student affairs will have a development officer within the institution's foundation assigned to focus on those functional areas or, in some cases, the student affairs division may have their own development officer on staff. Foundations recognize that student affairs professionals have a myriad of contacts and relationships (Morgan & Policello, 2010) that are ideal for cultivating gifts and will most likely be receptive to working with professionals (Puma, 2013).

The establishment of a fundraising program is often referred to as a campaign (Dove, 2001). A campaign will consist of an organized structure, an outlined plan, cultivation of donors intentionally from a top down approach, and it will be strategic (Dove, 2001). The key to working with the foundation will be to have a clear plan related to what is going to be funded and how much you are seeking. Foundation officers are most interested in talking about a specific program, service, or physical space that they can connect to prospective donors. Ensuring that the development officer has a clear understanding of the purpose and goals of the college union will be critical. Often the development officers will not understand the complexities of the college union organization. Professionals will need to be intentional about simplifying the message that will then be communicated to future donors. At this stage it will be critical for college union professionals to identify prospective donors that would be aligned with the "college union idea" (Butts, 1971). Considerations for prospective donors include former college union student leaders and employees, building managers, and families that have used college union facilities for major life events (e.g., weddings, anniversaries, etc.).

The challenge of working with an institutional foundation is that each project will be assigned a priority in relation to the additional campaigns that are being sought on campus. There are four distinct campaign models used today within higher education including the traditional annual campaign, capital campaign, comprehensive campaign, and the single-purpose campaign (Dove, 2001). The annual campaign solicits smaller gifts that will fund annual events throughout campus. This model is declining on college campuses and being replaced with more electronic fundraising efforts to capture the annual alumni giving. Annual giving programs on campus are run as independent organizations where students staff calling centers. The capital campaign solicits funds for large projects including campus buildings and often includes a number of larger campus priorities as the focus of the campaign. Historically, initiatives in college unions have been typically prioritized under capital campaigns related to new building construction or renovation (Puma, 2013). Today, college union professionals should consider a multi-pronged approach to fundraising, which recognizes that annual gifts and large endowments are both necessary for the advancement of programs and services. Puma (2013) pointed out that student affairs departments have the ability to connect to donors through affinity groups. Recognizing that students are engaged with their college union through employment opportunities and leadership roles offers a number of opportunities to cultivate donors. The use of private funds to support the advancement of programs and building projects will most likely continue to grow as part of the annual college union budget. Professionals in college unions will need to understand how to track students and document their college union's story for future giving.

Tracking Students for Future Giving.   Understanding what inspires students to be involved at the undergraduate level and give of their time would be a good indicator of what they may be willing to support with their time and funds as future donors (Gary & Adess, 2008). Keeping track of how former students were involved while they were attending the institution provides the initial connection in developing the donor relationship for a possible gift. Encouraging alumni to volunteer at events and programs is another way to engage and market future initiatives. Rarely will an organization be able to secure large donations during the first ask for a gift. Smaller gifts will also lead to larger gifts overtime (Drezner, 2011) and emphasize the importance of engagement with potential donors. Institutional alumni databases do not always capture the areas in which students were involved on campus. The databases are often linked to their academic department rather than their out-of-class activities. The establishment of a database of these students may or may not be something that can be done with the institutional foundation. It will be critical to ask questions related to who will maintain these data when setting up fundraising initiatives since not all institutions offer the same resources in relation to alumni data management. An intentional approach to fundraising on behalf of college unions will require a commitment to monitor and update potential donor information regularly.

Documenting the College Union Story.   Before asking for a gift, professionals in college unions need to be able to articulate the existing learning outcomes of current programs, services, and activities. Structures that support the capital campaign of new building construction or renovation are the foundation upon which professionals in college unions can build a case for the services they provide in those facilities. Puma (2013) pointed out that the cultivation of gifts for building projects may not be the focus for student affairs professionals, rather they should look how to capture the stories which will articulate the needs of students who will be using the facilities. Both donors and development officers need evidence that outlines how students are benefiting from being engaged in a college union, how they are contributing to the mission and vision of the institution, and how the students' involvement makes a difference.

Student Philanthropy in College Unions

Organized fundraising initiatives within college unions are not featured in the current literature. As a result, it is necessary to look at how higher education is engaging students in philanthropic activities that may increase their giving potential. Hurvitz (2010) researched how institutions in the Ivy-Plus consortium approach current students to create a culture of student philanthropy. Her findings emphasize the importance of campus culture in creating initiatives around fundraising that will be attractive to current students and connect them to their specific campus experiences. Creating the opportunity for student philanthropy requires an intentional approach that is focused on both student learning and future giving.

　　Student philanthropy is a teaching strategy that was established to create linkages between social needs and nonprofit organizations (Millisor & Olberding, 2009) and provides a potential framework for establishing a giving pattern with current students that are associated with their college union. Alumni provide an initial source; however, professionals in college unions must also cultivate current students as future donors.

　　As a learning laboratory, college unions have frameworks necessary to establish student philanthropy programs that would introduce students to this idea of "learning by giving" that has been growing within colleges and universities (Millisor & Olberding, 2009). Developing a student philanthropy model within college unions that engages students during their undergraduate years will set the stage for future giving. College unions have a unique opportunity to leverage the role of the union governing board to establish a student philanthropy model that exemplifies college unions' dedication to community service and town-gown relations.

　　The literature associated with student philanthropy is currently grounded in the academic curriculum or associated with larger direct giving programs (i.e., Campus Compact). Two primary models exist for the implementation of student philanthropy: (a) the direct giving model and (b) the indirect giving model (Olberding, 2009). The direct giving model provides funds to students, often from foundations or corporations, where students are then asked to invest those funds in a nonprofit organization.

Often associated with an academic course, students research nonprofits and ask organizations to submit grant proposals to review prior to making decisions related to where the direct funds given to the course will be distributed. The indirect model is inclusive of the review of grant proposals or requests from organizations for funds; however, the students only make recommendations and the sponsoring organization distributes the funding. Primarily used in the academic classroom, a few campuses have utilized the student philanthropy teaching strategy with student organizations on campus (Colgate University, n.d.; and Midland College, 2007, both as cited in Olberding, 2011).

Implementing a student philanthropy program within college unions could include the adoption of a direct giving model. College union governing or programming boards have often been involved in the strategic direction of college unions as student leaders. Adding an educational perspective of student philanthropy to the scope of the student group would engage these potential donors in how to responsibly use donor funds within college unions. Drezner (2013) found that involving students in fundraising provided them with the context for future giving. By utilizing the direct model of student philanthropy, student leaders could be given the opportunity to solicit and accept proposals from college union and/or campus community members on how to use a specified set of donor funds that were given to the college union. College union professionals could partner with their institution foundation to set up the initial gift and link the gift to the governing student organization in the college union. Fundraising professionals are aware that involvement on campus establishes a connection to the institution that can be cultivated into future giving (Puma, 2013). This model offers the unique opportunity for a college union to be a leader on campus in teaching students the value of "learning by giving" and position their college union as a future giving option for these students.

Olberding (2011) investigated the long-term effects of student philanthropy as a teaching strategy and discovered that students who participated in these programs were more likely to engage in the community and give to nonprofit organizations than those students who did not participate. The learning outcomes associated with student philanthropy models focus on (Olberding, 2009):

- increased understanding of philanthropic process including grant writing;
- integration of theory and practice related to philanthropy;
- awareness of nonprofits needs within the community;
- changes in how students approach the concepts of civic engagement and social responsibility; and
- improved critical thinking, communication, and leadership skills.

Transferring these general learning outcomes to college union contexts can be grounded in an understanding that students need to also recognize that their institution is a nonprofit organization. Knowing that their gift is going to make a difference and creating an opportunity for current and future students to have a similar experience make a compelling reason for donors contribute. Donors are looking for ways to say thank you and demonstrate their appreciation for their experiences (Gary & Adess, 2008). Establishing a student philanthropy model that is housed within a college union provides the opportunity for discussions and connections to the programmatic and facility needs within the collegiate environment. Last, this model can offer the opportunity for donors to designate a gift toward this learning activity.

Creating a Culture of Giving

Fundraising and philanthropy comprise a growing profession and area of research within higher education (Drezner, 2011). Research being conducted on giving to higher education has primarily examined donor behaviors (Harrison, 2008) and there is an emergence of literature calling for a more intentional approach to giving that is linked to theory and research (Drezner, 2011). Connections have been found between giving and involvement in student activities (Haddad, 1986; Hall, 1967; and Keller, 1982, all as cited in Harrison, 2008) and living on campus (Widick, 1985, as cited in Harrison, 2008). The more critical findings emerging from the literature highlight that future giving is linked to engaging students during their undergraduate experience with philanthropy and fundraising (Drezner, 2013; Hurvitz, 2010; Olberding, 2011).

Creating a culture of philanthropy is multifaceted and needs to include all the campus constituencies (Bennett, 2013). Establishing this culture of giving requires professionals in college unions to recognize and capitalize on the experiences that students are and will have within their facilities. Those experiences are often shared rituals and traditions that are unique to the institutional environment. Highlighting that tracking students associated with their affinity groups might prove to be beneficial in establishing future connections between students and alumni. The changing nature of professionals working in college unions will now most likely include the building of a brand community that will be able to articulate how to cultivate a culture of giving that is directed toward college unions.

References

Bennett, G. (2013). *Tips for weaving philanthropy into the campus fabric*. Retrieved from http://www.case.org/Publications_and_Products/2013/April_2013/The _Common_Thread.html

Butts, P. (1971). *The college union idea*. Stanford, CA: Association of College Unions International.

Conley, A., & Tempel, E. R. (2006). Philanthropy. In D. M. Priest & E. P. St. John (Eds.), *Privatization and public universities* (pp. 151–172). Bloomington: Indiana University Press.

Dove, K. E. (2001). *Conducting a successful fundraising program: A comprehensive guide and resource.* San Francisco, CA: Jossey-Bass.

Drezner, N. D. (2011). Philanthropy and fundraising in American higher education. *ASHE Higher Education Report, 37*(2). San Francisco, CA: Jossey-Bass.

Drezner, N. D. (Ed.). (2013). *Expanding the donor base in higher education: Engaging non-traditional donors.* New York, NY: Routledge.

Gary, T., & Adess, N. (2008). *Inspired philanthropy: Your step-by-step guide to creating a giving plan and leaving a legacy* (3rd ed.). San Francisco, CA: Jossey-Bass.

Harrison, W. B. (2008). College relations and fund-raising expenditures: Influencing the probability of alumni giving to higher education. In A. Walton & M. Gasman (Eds.), *Philanthropy, volunteerism, & fundraising in higher education* (pp. 672–685). Boston, MA: Pearson Custom Publishing.

Hurvitz, L. A. (2010). *Building a culture of student philanthropy: A study of the Ivy-Plus institutions' philanthropy education initiatives* (Dissertation). University of Pennsylvania, Philadelphia, PA. (UMI No. 3410478)

Kaplan, A. E. (2013). *2012 Voluntary support of education.* New York, NY: Council for Aid to Education.

Miller, T. E. (Ed.). (2010). *New Directions for Student Services: No. 130. Advancement work in student affairs: The challenges and strategies.* San Francisco, CA: Jossey-Bass.

Millisor, J., & Olberding, J. C. (2009). Student philanthropy in college and universities. *Academic Exchange Quarterly, 13*(4), 11–16.

Morgan, M. F., & Policello, S. M. (2010). Getting started in student affairs development. In T. E. Miller (Ed.), *New Directions for Student Services: No. 130. Advancement work in student affairs: The challenges and strategies* (pp. 9–18). San Francisco, CA: Jossey-Bass.

Olberding, J. C. (2009). Indirect giving to nonprofit organizations: An emerging model of student philanthropy. *Journal of Public Affairs Education, 15*(4), 463–492.

Olberding, J. C. (2011). Does student philanthropy work? A study of long-term effects of the "learning by giving" approach. *Innovative Higher Education, 37*(2), 71–87. Retrieved from http://www.trincoll.edu/Academics/centers/teaching/Documents/Week%208%20--%20Does%20Student%20Philanthropy%20Work.pdf

Puma, M. (2013). Fostering student affairs and institutional advancement partnerships. In N. D. Drezner (Ed.), *Expanding the donor base in higher education: Engaging non-traditional donors* (pp. 171–186). San Francisco, CA: Jossey-Bass.

Schuh, J. H. (2011). Financing student affairs. In J. H. Schuh, S. R. Jones, S. R. Harper, & Associates (Eds.), *Student services: A handbook for the profession* (5th ed., pp. 303–320). San Francisco, CA: Jossey-Bass.

DANIELLE M. DE SAWAL *is a clinical associate professor and coordinator of the Higher Education and Student Affairs master's program at Indiana University.*

DANIEL MAXWELL *is associate vice chancellor and associate vice president for Student Affairs at the University of Houston.*

6

This chapter examines how college union professionals can keep up with changes in technology and address student expectations regarding information technology.

Impact and Evolution of Technology in College Unions

John Taylor, Rich Steele

Today's college students have grown up in a world immersed in technology, so much so that it has become an essential part of their daily life (Martinez Aleman & Wartman, 2009). Their familiarity and use of technology is strong, with 86% having a computer prior to coming to college, 88% owning a cell phone, and 88% accessing the Internet daily (Student Monitor, 2013). Students enter college with an increased understanding of how to use technology tools and are considered to be one of the most Internet-active groups in the United States (Jones, 2002). Recognizing the increasing use of technology by students, it is important for professionals working in college unions to be as current as possible in the technology arena and to understand student expectations regarding information technology (IT).

College union facilities have provided a venue for the use of technology on campus with examples that date to the early twentieth century. At the Oxford Union, a telegram board was used by the campus community to share news and events and a photographic dark room was available for community use in Houston Hall at the University of Pennsylvania (Butts et al., 2012). Directors of the college union have consistently considered the role of technology within the physical building design, as evidenced by Porter Butts's 1938 description of the Wisconsin Union, "When we open the new rooms, we open also new frontiers... in the special technique of radio drama, in the making as well as the showing of sound moving pictures" (Butts et al., 2012, p. 60). Over the years, the greatest challenge for professionals in college unions has been to stay current with technology and students' use of technology. For example, college campuses in the 1990s were barely able to fund Ethernet in college union facilities when technology and student standards advanced to a new wireless platform. College union professionals, however, continue to recognize the importance of using technology as a valuable tool in the delivery of programs, services, and cocurricular educational experiences. In 2005, the Association of College Unions

NEW DIRECTIONS FOR STUDENT SERVICES, no. 145, Spring 2014 © 2014 Wiley Periodicals, Inc.
Published online in Wiley Online Library (wileyonlinelibrary.com) • DOI: 10.1002/ss.20080

International (ACUI, 2012) identified technology as one of the eleven core competencies for the profession. The use of technology in higher education has provided the opportunity for the creation of "communities for work, play, and learning in ways unimaginable [over] a decade ago" (Duderstadt, Atkins, & Van Houweling, 2006, Preface). McElvain and Smyth (2006) emphasized that using technology as an educational tool enhances engagement and learning. This calls attention to the fact that professionals working in college unions need to adapt technology that encourages the college union's role as a campus community builder.

Overall, professionals in the field of student affairs are typically less familiar with the new methods of technology than students (Junco & Cole-Avent, 2008), especially those associated with using social media as a form of communication (Junco & Mastrodicasa, 2007; Martinez Aleman & Wartman, 2011). Student affairs professionals have recognized for more than a decade that the students attending college expect a sophisticated level of technology to be used throughout their collegiate experience (Blimling, 2000). This is further validated by the recognition that technology is considered a core competency by student affairs professional associations (ACPA/NASPA, 2010; ACUI, 2012). Professionals working in college unions need to be aware of how technology can be a partner in increasing student engagement in relation to both the operation of college union facilities and programming initiatives, given that the intentional use of technology has been linked to an increase in student engagement (Astin, 1999; Hu & Kuh, 2001; Nelson Laird & Kuh, 2005). This chapter explores the impact of technology on college unions and offers practical solutions for using technology to enhance both the operational efficiency of the facility and student programming engagement.

Facility Operations

A college union's physical building can range from historic structures with an antiquated infrastructure to buildings recently constructed that house the most up-to-date technology. Whether updating an existing building or planning for a new facility, technology solutions are available to maximize guest satisfaction and Internet access, building efficiency and sustainability, and improve the campus community's safety within the facility. The technology solutions that are found within a college union's facility range from energy efficient infrastructures to web-based reservations systems that are available to simplify access for the entire campus community. The technology systems that enhance the environmental conditions (e.g., room temperature, lighting, etc.) are frequently not visible to the public, rather they are the aspects of college union operation that create a comfortable place to learn and socialize. Systems that support remote monitoring and control of heating, ventilation, and air conditioning (HVAC) can provide data that inform preventive maintenance plans and optimize building performance.

NEW DIRECTIONS FOR STUDENT SERVICES • DOI: 10.1002/ss

The use of data from these types of information technology systems has changed the management and administrative processes within higher education throughout the institution (Duderstadt et al., 2006).

The recent emphasis to achieve Leadership in Energy and Environmental Design (LEED®) certification with campus buildings has prompted attention on energy management and building automation. Institutions seeking LEED® certification for campus buildings want to demonstrate a conscious effort to minimize the impact of the buildings lifecycle on the environment (Lange & Kerr, 2013). The five environmental criteria that are associated with LEED® certification include: sustainable site; water efficiency; energy and atmosphere; materials and resources; and indoor environmental quality. Within college union facilities that are LEED® certified, technology tools that are used to support sustainable practice include occupancy and photo sensors that create automated illumination to reduce energy consumption when a room is not in use. Advances in lamp technology offer retrofit and new installation options for energy efficient lighting using compact fluorescent (CFL) and light-emitting diode (LED) lamps. Automated window shades control the effect of sunlight on ambient indoor conditions. Tools that monitor and display power consumption in real time also encourage behavioral change with end users and facility managers to reduce consumption. These intelligent building systems also require facility maintenance and operations staff who are able to operate more complex and computer-driven systems. This shift in personnel requirements for operational staff within college unions will also impact the focus of some of those positions to be more grounded in skills and knowledge associated with information technology.

More than ever, security is an important issue on college campuses, and college union professionals need to recognize that as a public facility, they must balance the expectation of providing an accessible and comfortable environment for the campus community with the need for increased security for those individuals using the building. Crime and violence on campus has become more prevalent and college campuses need to create an environment where there is perceived to be effective security (Chekwa, Thomas, & Jones, 2013). Monitoring the people who enter and leave a college union can be challenging. Two common tools available to monitor access include card access systems and security cameras. While many college unions have open doors during regular operating hours, a card access system allows for better security during off hours. Designated cardholders, such as student organization officers, can gain access to the building or an office through approval provided on their access card, often the campus ID. Similarly, security cameras can be strategically placed to monitor and record entrances or certain areas of a college union. Both security solutions are commonplace in public venues such as hotels, retail stores, and other campus facilities (e.g., residence halls and academic buildings).

New Directions for Student Services • DOI: 10.1002/ss

Technology systems within a college union also control the access and speed at which the campus community can access their personal technology tools within the facility. With students, faculty, and staff expecting wireless access during meetings and events, professionals in college unions need to be aware of how to meet the expanding demands for the individual use of technology. In 2012, the Georgia Tech Student Center upgraded network switches and wireless access points to accommodate student demand for faster and better wireless coverage. The speed of wireless access points is based on the current IEEE standard of 802.11n ("n" signifying theoretical speeds up to 300 megabits per second). Bandwidth, the maximum data transfer rate, is also impacted by network switches and other hardware/wiring. Generally, student Internet consumption in 2013 called for gigabit Ethernet switches, which better met student desire to simultaneously connect two wireless devices, typically a laptop/tablet and a smartphone, when utilizing college union facilities. In the case of Georgia Tech, wireless network coverage was accomplished with 41 access points (increased from 17) over a 150,000 square foot facility. Access points were installed with greater density in locations with higher density seating or the potential for large audiences.

A significant role in many of the college unions in the United States is the management of conferences and events. Technology tools have enhanced this function, allowing for greater efficiencies by professionals in college unions in the planning and delivery of standard meetings as well as complex events. The age of reserving rooms in a hardbound ledger is long gone, with most scheduling managed through software and online access for clients, such as Event Management System (EMS), Resource 25, and Ungerboeck Software. These programs are set up to specifically house the details (e.g., square footage and furniture options) associated with each room within a college union. Details ranging from room setup, catering menu selection, and audio visual (AV) needs can be easily requested, confirmed, and changed by professionals. Such software also allows for better customer service and efficiency. Computer room diagramming, for example, helps the client to visualize their event, reduces the possibility of setup mistakes, and confirms in advance whether a desired furniture arrangement will adequately fit in a room.

The Future Role of the Campus Bookstore and Retail Venues

Over the years there have been various retail services in college unions, some that have thrived and others that have disappeared. College unions often house a variety of retail services that are available to the campus community and are frequently driven by community need and current retail trends within society. For example, the U.S. Education Secretary Arne Duncan stated that printed textbooks would be obsolete in the near future due to e-books and digital readers (von Glahn, 2013). This emergence of digital technology has greatly challenged the textbook industry (McDermott, North, Meszaros, Caywood, & Danzell, 2011), bringing into question the role of the conventional campus bookstore, often found in college unions.

The University of Michigan assessed the future of the campus bookstore through interviews with public K–12 school administrators, higher education focus groups, and the analysis of media reports and industry trends. This revealed that serious technology enhancements have and will continue to alter the traditional college bookstore, with its future in question. The younger (grade school) generation is adapting well to new technology, suggesting a stronger affinity to resources, such as electronic readers, than current college students. While hard copy textbooks are still common for today's college students (McDermott et al., 2011), affordability will be a factor in the consideration for campuses transitioning to alternative electronic resources. Online textbook rentals, for example, provide students a less expensive option to obtain electronic course material on a short-term basis, and open source textbooks, which can be altered by faculty for their specific classes, provide a free resource for students to use online. There is no doubt that changes in the delivery of educational content will affect the purpose of the campus bookstore.

Conducting retail business over the Internet, or e-commerce, is a common service offering on college campuses. For example, campus bookstores typically offer their inventory of institutional logo clothing, gifts, supplies, and course materials online expanding the potential sales reach to include alumni. Links between online course registration systems and e-commerce textbook sites introduce a valued element of convenience for students buying required course materials. For example, Indiana University offers faculty the option of requiring e-textbooks that are then automatically added to the students bursar account when the student registers for the course. The campus community can also benefit from special access to e-commerce sites via authentication tools using university credentials, which allows customers to take advantage of negotiated discounts and special offers.

Technology tools can aid campus dining operations housed in a college union that struggle with overcrowding at peak intervals due to an influx of customers seeking food or coffee between classes and at primary meal periods. Mobile solutions have been introduced in the university environment to support remote ordering and payment to reduce wait times and increase sales. Additionally, unattended cash register systems have proven effective to increase customer throughput without increasing labor costs. For example, a Georgia Tech fast casual restaurant increased throughput of customers by nearly 10%, saved 33% in cashier labor costs, and increased the average purchase by 7%.

Student Organization Advising

Student involvement is a critical component to student success (Astin, 1999). The role of technology within the physical structure of a college union often shadows the role technology plays in creating the conditions necessary to engage students in the campus programming college unions offer. Professionals working directly with student organizations are often stretched for time, expending efforts on transactional interactions that revolve around the logistics of recognizing a student organization on campus. This detracts from a more significant advising role, noted as encouraging student learning and development (Love & Maxam, 2011). Technological tools, however, can enhance an advisor's ability to engage students more effectively and support student organizations, and create more time for relationship building.

A recent technological solution on college campuses is the use of cocurricular or student organization content management systems. Such resources provide "back of the house" data management for the student activities/organization office and seamless online access and resources for students. Content management systems, such as Collegiate Link, Symplicity, and Org Sync, typically offer the following types of resources:

Registration. An online process that captures organizational data.
Email. The ability for distribution options to push communication out to student organization officers, members, and subgroups.
Cocurricular transcript. Students can document their involvement and out of classroom experience.
Web pages. Student organizations can set up a web page through the management system and/or linking to their existing organizational web page.
Finances. Student organization finances can be managed with the institution's financial system, including online funding requests and account balances.
Student involvement. Event and involvement opportunities can be promoted to students.
Event assessment. Attendance can be tracked and online surveys created.
Rosters. Advisors or student organization leaders can manage membership lists, send out emails, and categorize involvement.

Also, a college union may operate movie programs, theaters, and performing arts venues that benefit from in-house box office capabilities and a software solution to sell and print tickets. Such systems typically support season ticketing, group discounts, customer accounts, communications, fundraising, and audit trail accounting for handling funds and ticket stock. Campus card systems provide tools to automate event access through electronic ticketing or verification of fee payment. Utilizing an online marketplace, such as Touchnet® and Sequoia Retail Systems ePOS, card systems can automate ticket purchases and store transactions that can be verified electronically utilizing handheld or installed access readers. This technology reduces the cost of ticket printing and handling, and eliminates the risk of inventory shrinkage. It also allows students to use their campus ID as verification of an e-ticket for admission to a specific event. These technology tools, which are frequently linked to the response of the millennial generations desire for immediate gratification, provide the opportunity for engaging students differently on campus (Lowery, 2004) and provide data to evaluate programs and services offered by a college union.

Marketing

Marketing the services and opportunities in a college union has moved far beyond advertising in the campus newspaper, to avenues such as digital displays, an effective web presence, and social media. Digital displays are becoming more common for effectively communicating to building patrons. Using connected system software allows information from multiple resources to be automatically pulled and displayed on building screens. For example, college union managers can display building events from EMS, highlight services, and broadcast emergency alerts from the campus police department. Digital displays can be a very effective visual tool, whether advertising retail services offered in the college union, displaying food vendor specials, or providing means to navigate the college union building. These digital displays can also be interactive, providing an opportunity for students to engage the display to specifically locate information that is pertinent to them. When connected to the broader campus information technology infrastructure digital displays in the college union can also be accessed by campus safety personnel to extend notification of important information in the event of an emergency.

Websites serve as the online brand identity of an organization and should reflect the same visual imagery and quality standards evident in the physical space of an organization. While a well-designed website is an important marketing tool, customers will need motivation and ease of access to navigate the site. Navigational links to social media, including image and video sharing, are common and can enhance attraction to the site. Online visitors expect to experience information, images, and services in a logical format for their daily lives and not to be forced into following virtual breadcrumbs based on organizational structures that are only meaningful to insiders. The main website page should display the organization's name, address, phone number, and basic operational information. Professionals in college unions will want to work directly with their informational technology services offices to ensure that branding and the internal structure of the website meet institutional guidelines. Professionals should also be

NEW DIRECTIONS FOR STUDENT SERVICES • DOI: 10.1002/ss

aware that data from web analytics can be used to assess the effectiveness of communication, social media usage, and services offered.

When marketing a college union, it is important to understand that traditional college-age students fall into the "millennial" generational category, individuals born after 1982, considered to be coming of age in the new millennium (Strauss & Howe, 2006). According to a Pew Research Center (2010) report on "millennial students," technology clearly plays an important role in their lives, and differently than other generations. "It's not just their gadgets—it's the way they've fused their social lives into them" (p. 13). In a number of areas, but especially social networking, millennial students far outpace older generations in their use of social networking sites such as Facebook.

There is little question that students operate in a world where Facebook, Twitter, and YouTube are an important part of how they carry out their everyday activities. In fact, 95% of entering freshmen reported spending time on social network sites (Pryor, DeAngelo, Palucki Blake, Hurtado, & Tran, 2011). College union professionals must look for ways to intentionally engage students through social media because operating in sync with students provides an access point for student involvement. For example, effectively using social media provides opportunities for students to connect not just with each other but also with the campus activities office to learn how to become involved on campus. Being familiar with and intentional in using social media provides different avenues for an advisor to engage with students, to learn of their interests, and to best support student organization endeavors. College union staff must reimagine their traditional functions in a new light. For example, the traditional role of the college union information desk is to disseminate information. Effectively using social media allows for two-way, rather than one-way, communication. For example, the information desk attendants could monitor social media on campus, pushing out content based on trends and what is being discussed, rather than waiting to be asked a one-on-one question at the physical desk.

Interestingly, even though students are heavily engaged in online social networks, this has not limited their involvement on campus, and in fact the opposite may be true. According to Heiberger and Harper (2008), 94% of students reported using social networks weekly and spent no less time studying or participating in cocurricular activities than students who do not use social networks. The authors also indicated that students who more frequently use social networks also spend more time in campus activities such as student organizations. Similarly, a Higher Education Research Institute (2007) brief noted a positive correlation between social networking website use and college student engagement, with heavy users indicating more frequent daily interaction with close friends and strong connections to them.

NEW DIRECTIONS FOR STUDENT SERVICES • DOI: 10.1002/ss

Planning for the Future

Intel cofounder Gordon Moore is associated with the concept that the processing power for computers will double every two years. Moore's law (Intel Corporation, 2005), as the concept has been termed, alludes to the speed at which technology changes, and the challenge of staying current. Recognizing this dilemma, here are some practical applications for professionals working in college unions to consider in planning for the "near" future.

Cloud computing describes the Internet as a "cloud" providing services that can replace the functionality of personal computers in terms of storage, software, and even platform functionality. Remote server storage offers broadly scalable, hosted solutions for web services, file storage, or software sharing and can fulfill the need for off-site data backup. The cost of cloud storage is offset by eliminating the need for staff to maintain onsite services and by eliminating cyclical hardware replacement costs. Software as a Service (SaaS) describes a cloud computing scenario that delivers software solutions via a compatible browser rather than installed on individual devices. A common example of SaaS is Google Docs, which provides software compatible with the Microsoft Office suite and file storage for shared documents. Broad adoption of cloud computing is considered inevitable in business as a cost-saving measure, viewed as outsourcing of technology assets (Monaco, 2012). Local storage of critical files is recommended to avoid loss of business continuity due to network failure or inaccessibility.

Tablet computers offer a mobile platform with sufficient digital real estate to effectively view large and complex data formats. Facility operations staff in the college union at Florida State University (Watson & Wuest, 2012) adopted tablet computers and document sharing to view setup worksheets, share photographs for maintenance work orders, and to complete shift reports. This initiative resulted in cost savings, more accurate setup information, and more effective communications. One limitation observed was the difficulty of handling the tablet computer while also fulfilling the manual workload required for room setup.

A smartphone is defined as "a mobile phone offering advanced capabilities, often with PC-like functionality or able to download apps" (Google/IPSOS OTX MediaCT, 2011, p. 3). The proliferation of these devices on campus opens a new world of opportunity and challenge. Strategies specific to smartphone platforms, the user audience, and content format are necessary to capitalize on the opportunity to interact with students regardless of location. A Google/IPSOS OTX MediaCT (2011) study identified that 89% of online adults age 18–64 used their smartphone throughout the day. Most (89%) used their devices for e-mail and social media, 82% indicated that they experienced a mobile advertisement, and nearly half were called to action because of the ad (visit website, visit store, and make purchase). While potentially enticing to college union marketing professionals, thorough planning is required before assuming the cost and complexity of addressing the mobile student through websites designed for smaller screens and finger navigation, or through a customized smartphone app.

Professionals in college unions must acknowledge the limited useful life of technology assets and plan for the financial impact of their replacement. The generally accepted life cycle for computers is 3–4 years, for displays and projectors 5–7 years, and for audio systems 10–15 years. Straight-line depreciation is sufficient for most technologies as costs tend to decrease over time, especially for computer hardware. Annual maintenance for technology assets should be budgeted at 5–8% of the equipment value.

The cost of professional IT staff continues to rise at a faster pace than most other higher education specialties. First quarter 2013 indices show that IT staff pay is up 5.1% over prior year while administrative and clerical staff pay was half that increase (2.6%) over the same period (PayScale, 2013). The level of expertise and the breadth of services that require IT staff involvement is also growing at a fast pace. Departments may require more in-house staff to manage complex web services, e-commerce sites, social media coordination, and AV technology. IT leadership staff play an increasingly dominant role in establishing and managing the strategic direction of organizations. This growth of IT expenses must be considered in planning the budget of a college union.

Conclusion

While it is important for professionals in college unions to understand student technology use and incorporate related applications into programs and services, such an effort is recognized as fairly complex (Junco & Cole-Avent, 2008). Proficiency in the core competency area of technology is important, just as is putting a comprehensive and effective technology strategy in place. By embracing technology, college union professionals can expand student involvement opportunities and operate more efficient facilities while reducing costs. There is no denying the challenges involved with "staying current," as technology advances at a very fast pace. However, professionals in college unions must continue to develop in the technology arena to engage students through contemporary means and to respond to evolving campus needs.

References

American College Personnel Association & National Association of Student Personnel Administrators (ACPA/NASPA). (2010). *ACPA/NASPA professional competency areas for student affairs practitioners.* Washington, DC: Author.

Association of College Unions International (ACUI). (2012). *Core competencies for the college union and student activities profession.* Retrieved from http://www.acui .org/content.aspx?menu_id=30&id=9463

Astin, A. W. (1999). Student involvement: A developmental theory for higher education. *Journal of College Student Development, 40*(5), 518–529.

Blimling, G. S. (2000). New technologies: Changing how we work with students. *About Campus, 5*(4), 3–7.

Butts, P., Beltramini, E., Bourassa, M., Connelly, P., Meyer, R., Mitchell, S., ... Willis, T. J. (Eds.). (2012). *The college union idea* (2nd ed.). Bloomington, IN: Association of College Unions International.

Chekwa, C., Thomas, E., Jr., & Jones, V. J. (2013). What are college students' perceptions about campus safety? *Contemporary Issues in Education Research, 6*(3), 325–332.

Duderstadt, J. J., Atkins, D. E., & Van Houweling, D. (2006). *Higher education in the digital age: Technology issues and strategies for American colleges and universities.* Westport, CT: American Council on Education and Praeger Publishers.

Google/IPSOS OTX MediaCT. (2011). *The mobile movement.* Retrieved from http://ssl.gstatic.com/think/docs/the-mobile-movement_research-studies.pdf

Heiberger, G., & Harper, R. (2008). Have you Facebooked Astin lately? Using technology to increase student involvement. In R. Junco & D. M. Timm (Eds.), *New Directions for Student Services: No. 124. Using emerging technologies to enhance student engagement* (pp. 19–35). San Francisco, CA: Jossey-Bass.

Higher Education Research Institute. (2007). *College freshmen and online social networking sites.* Retrieved from http://www.gseis.ucla.edu/heri/PDFs/pubs/briefs/brief-091107-SocialNetworking.pdf

Hu, S., & Kuh, G. D. (2001). Computing experience and good practices in undergraduate education: Does the degree of campus "Wiredness" matter? *Education Policy Analysis Archives, 9*(49). Retrieved from http://epaa.asu.edu/epaa/v9n49.html

Intel Corporation. (2005). *Excerpts from a conversation with Gordon Moore: Moore's law.* Retrieved from http://large.stanford.edu/courses/2012/ph250/lee1/docs/Excepts_A_Conversation_with_Gordon_Moore.pdf

Jones, S. (2002). *The Internet goes to college: How students are living in the future with today's technology.* Washington, DC: Pew Internet and American Life Project.

Junco, R., & Cole-Avent, G. A. (2008). An introduction to technologies commonly used by college students. In R. Junco & D. M. Timm (Eds.), *New Directions for Student Services: No. 124. Using emerging technologies to enhance student engagement* (pp. 3–17). San Francisco, CA: Jossey-Bass.

Junco, R., & Mastrodicasa, J. (2007). *Connecting to the net generation: What higher education professionals need to know about today's students.* Washington, DC: National Association of Student Personnel Administrators.

Lange, E. A., & Kerr, S. G. (2013). Accounting and incentives for sustainability in higher education: An interdisciplinary analysis of a needed revolution. *Social Responsibility Journal, 9*(2), 210–219.

Love, P., & Maxam, S. (2011). Advising and consultation. In J. H. Schuh, S. R. Jones, S. R. Harper, & Associates (Eds.), *Student services: A handbook for the profession* (5th ed., pp. 413–432). San Francisco, CA: Jossey-Bass.

Lowery, J. W. (Ed.). (2004). *New Directions for Student Services: No. 106. Student affairs for a new generation.* San Francisco, CA: Jossey-Bass.

Martinez Aleman, A. M., & Wartman, K. L. (2009). *Online social networking on campus: Understanding what matters in student culture.* New York, NY: Routledge.

Martinez Aleman, A. M., & Wartman, K. L. (2011). Assessment and evaluation. In J. H. Schuh, S. R. Jones, S. R. Harper, & Associates (Eds.), *Student services: A handbook for the profession* (5th ed., pp. 515–533). San Francisco, CA: Jossey-Bass.

McDermott, J., North, P., Meszaros, G., Caywood, J. A., & Danzell, L. (2011). Exploring the path of bookstore trends. *NACAS College Services, 11*(4), 16–23.

McElvain, K., & Smyth, C. (2006). Facebook: Implications for student affairs professionals. *The Bulletin, 74*(2), 18–22.

Monaco, A. (2012). *A view inside the cloud.* Retrieved from http://theinstitute
.ieee.org/technology-focus/technology-topic/a-view-inside-the-cloud

Nelson Laird, T. F., & Kuh, G. D. (2005). Student experiences with information technology and their relationship to other aspects of student engagement. *Research in Higher Education, 46*(2), 211–233.

PayScale. (2013). *Pay trends for information technology jobs.* Retrieved from http://www.payscale.com/payscale-index-Q1-2013/job-categories/information
-technology-jobs

Pew Research Center. (2010). *Millennials: Confident. Connected. Open to change.* Washington DC: Author.

Pryor, J. H., DeAngelo, L., Palucki Blake, L., Hurtado, S., & Tran, S. (2011). *The American freshman: National norms fall 2011.* Los Angeles, CA: Higher Education Research Institute, UCLA.

Strauss, W., & Howe, N. (2006). *Millennials and the pop culture: Strategies for a new generation of consumers in music, movies, television, the Internet, and video games.* Great Falls, VA: LifeCourse Associates.

Student Monitor. (2013). Retrieved from http://www.studentmonitor.com

von Glahn, M. (2013). Plug in: How to market and sell digital course materials. *The College Store, 80*(1), 22–30.

Watson, M., & Wuest, M. (2012, November). *Integrating iPads into union operations.* Paper presented at the Region 6 Conference of the Association of College Unions International, Tallahassee, FL.

JOHN TAYLOR *is the senior director of Auxiliary Services and director of University Unions at the University of Michigan.*

RICH STEELE *is the senior director of Auxiliary Services at Georgia Institute of Technology.*

7

This chapter examines the current state of college unions at small colleges and offers a forecast of their future.

Small College Unions

Ian Crone, Eric Tammes

Small colleges have a historic role in higher education; they include a vast diversity of missions and constituencies and compose the majority of higher education institutions in the United States (Westfall, 2006a). Small colleges are often described as having a more meaningful and supportive sense of community than their larger peers. Thus, it is crucial to consider the role of a college union within a small college. While there are a couple of books that provide insights into the work of student affairs administrators on small colleges (see Westfall's [2006b] *The Small College Dean: New Directions for Student Services* and Kuh & McAleenan's [1986] *Private Dreams, Shared Visions: Student Affairs Work in Small Colleges*), little is written that specifically explores the role, impact, and future of college unions at small colleges. This chapter examines the current state of college unions at small colleges and offers a forecast of their future.

Defining Small Colleges

Small colleges in the United States encompass many institutional classifications: urban, rural, public, private, religious-affiliated, secular, two-year, four-year, historically black, tribal, and single sex. Westfall (2006a) asserted that "size matters"; what small colleges have in common is the size of their student bodies. Carnegie Classification and higher education professional associations provide measurements that define a very small two-year institution as having a full-time equivalent (FTE) enrollment of less than 500 students and a small two-year institution with an FTE of 500–1,999 students. At the four-year level, a very small institution is defined as having less than 1,000 FTE and a small institution as enrolling 1,000–2,999 FTE (Carnegie, 2012).

An institution's size informs the services, programs, and membership levels available from professional associations. The Association of College Unions International (ACUI) determined "the functional definition of 'small school' consistent with ACUI membership categories is full-time

NEW DIRECTIONS FOR STUDENT SERVICES, no. 145, Spring 2014 © 2014 Wiley Periodicals, Inc.
Published online in Wiley Online Library (wileyonlinelibrary.com) • DOI: 10.1002/ss.20081

equivalent enrollment of 5,000 students or less" (ACUI, 2012, para. 2). The National Orientation Directors Association (NODA) uses an identical measure of 5,000 students to define NODA's small college network (NODA, 2013). Full-time equivalent enrollment of 4,000 or fewer students sets the small institutions membership level for the National Association of College and University Business Officers (NACUBO, 2013). For the purposes of this chapter, a small college is an institution with an FTE of 5,000 students or less.

History of Small Colleges

Small colleges assume a central role in the history of higher education in the United States. A majority of institutions prior to World War II would have been defined as small, yet they collectively educated most baccalaureate degree-seeking students (Westfall, 2006a). Small colleges were plentiful, particularly in rural areas, during the 1800s through the 1940s. Support from religions denominations, affordability of land, growth of rail service, and westward expansion fueled the chartering of small colleges. As enrollments swelled into the 1950s and 1960s, land grant and state universities expanded and the balance of enrollment shifted to larger institutions.

Now, small colleges are challenged to maintain enrollment, thereby causing institutions to wrestle with finding the ideal institutional size to deliver a quality education and meet increasing financial demands and challenges (Fain, 2005). Many students and their families are drawn to public institutions that offer lower tuition rates in a price-conscious marketplace (Hoover, 2005). Many small colleges have closed, merged, and dramatically changed educational offerings as public demand for higher education has evolved.

The history of college unions on small college campuses is largely absent from the literature. In the touchstone college union publication, *The College Union Idea*, Porter Butts (1971) offers few references to small colleges. References to the history of small college unions are primarily found in small school histories and reveal that the core function for the college union facilities were originally functional needs, such as student dining.

Here are some examples of the focus on functionality. Elmhurst College built the Commons in 1896 to serve as dining hall and kitchen, laundry, sick room, guest rooms, and an apartment for the superintendent and was replaced by the college union in 1964 (Cutright, 1995). A former president of Buena Vista University raised funds to construct a new school of business facility that incorporated college union functions, such as a cafeteria, bookstore, and student activities office, into a four-acre underground facility that opened in 1985 (Cumberland, 1991). Students from Valparaiso University raised a student fee to build the first Valparaiso Union in 1951 (Strietelmeier, 1959). Ripon College's Harwood Memorial Union was constructed in 1942 to provide a modern dining facility, featuring family style dining, in addition to a student lounge, admissions office, and student organization office spaces. Twenty years later, a new dining facility was constructed to meet the needs of a growing student body and the Harwood Union dining hall was converted into a multipurpose room (Ripon College, 2013).

Institutions of all sizes are committed to their academic missions. However, mission and values are intricately, and often intensely, intertwined with day-to-day experiences throughout all areas of a small college. Mission matters at small colleges, particularly in maintaining enrollment, creating distinction in the marketplace, decision making, and determining staff and faculty needs (Heida, 2006). McDonald & Associates (2002) found that "responses from students from small schools affirmed that their institution's mission and purpose affected them daily. Students' responses from large schools were neutral and did not indicate such an impact in their lives" (p. 154). The intersection of people and institutional mission ultimately creates a small college environment with distinctive characteristics and attributes (Kuh & McAleenan, 1986). A college union at a small college can be positioned to support the institutional mission through programming, space use, staff training and development, and community building.

Physical Space: Clearly Defined or Intentionally Blended

A college union in a small college seeks to unite its college community, providing services and self-directed activities intended to support the institution's educational mission (ACUI, 1996). However, while their role is consistent with that of college unions at large institutions, the physical characteristics of unions at small colleges vary widely. Some small colleges have college unions that represent the traditional model of a contemporary union outlined by the Council for the Advancement of Standards (CAS) in *Higher Education Self-Assessment Guide for College Unions*. These unions combine community space, such as lounges and meeting space, with services, such as dining spaces and bookstores, and space for student engagement and leisure (CAS, 2009).

Other college unions at small colleges may promote community with little or no physical space due to financial and structural limitations. *The Role of the College Union* suggests that physical space is not necessary for the college union; what is necessary is a commitment by the campus to building community, engaging students, and forming connections (ACUI, 1996).

Roosevelt University represents this latter model. An urban university with an undergraduate enrollment of 2,900, Roosevelt University's downtown Chicago campus occupies two historic academic buildings and a 32-story skyscraper, the second tallest building on a U.S. college campus. Absent a bricks and mortar union building, the role of the college union at

Roosevelt University is fulfilled by a student involvement program employing lounges and programming space throughout the glass covered "vertical campus" (Roosevelt University, 2013).

Another example is St. Norbert College in De Pere, Wisconsin, which has an enrollment of just over 2,000. Renovated in 1999, the Ray Van Den Heuvel Family Campus Center combines a fitness center and basketball courts with more traditional aspects of a college union, such as a café, programming space, student organizational offices, and lounge space (ACUI, 2008).

In contrast, the Marbeck Center, serving as a campus center for Bluffton University, a small private college in Ohio, represents a more traditional model described by the CAS standards. The Marbeck Center includes lounge and meeting space, and consolidating dining and student mail services, meeting space and student involvement and orientation office space, as well as offices for conference services (Bourassa, 2012). Similarly, the Knobloch Campus Center provides the 1,700 students of Davidson College (NC) with many amenities of the traditional union model, including a bookstore and copy center, fitness facilities, a performance hall and dining facilities, career services, student organizational office space, and the campus chaplain (Davidson College, 2012). Ultimately, although the physical characteristics of college unions at small colleges can vary widely, the use of space for building community is consistent with the college unions found at large institutions.

Small colleges will continue to create spaces that are most appropriate to the campus culture and institutional needs. Blended spaces may be more desirable as colleges consider how to create effective learning environments with physical and financial constraints. An example is North Park University in Chicago. Home to 1,900 undergraduates, the University will open a new science and campus life center in 2014, combining science labs, campus ministries, career development, classrooms, and a café (North Park University, 2013). This unique combination of spaces reflects the institution's educational needs and commitment to building community.

Small Union Staffing: Wearers of Many Hats

One way that small college unions differ from those at larger institutions is the scale and organization of their staffs. Often, the student affairs administrators who manage and lead college unions at small colleges are responsible for additional functional areas, such as student activities, fraternity and sorority life, leadership programs, campus scheduling, and summer conferences and events (Heida, 2006). For these college union professionals, the need to be a generalist, and wear many professional hats, can be both a limitation and an opportunity. For example, Oblander (2006) described how the generally flat organizational structure at a small college can provide greater access to key decision makers on campus than at larger institutions

NEW DIRECTIONS FOR STUDENT SERVICES • DOI: 10.1002/ss

and can lead to a greater ability to collaborate and innovate. Yet some of the advantages of the small school generalist role, coupled with more frequent interactions with students, can contribute to a "grand delusion of being a superstar or a 'hero'" (Goffigon, Lacey, Wright, & Kuh, 1986, pp. 97–98). For small college administrators, these pressures can lead to burn out.

In addition, small staff size can limit opportunities for professional advancement within the organization and can also make it harder for new staff to learn the culture and negotiate campus politics, as policies and expectations are often informal or unarticulated (Oblander, 2006). Given the limited ability for advancement that is often found at a small college, junior professionals often occupy front line roles, such as assistant directors who are responsible for student activities, college union operations, or both. Oblander (2006) described how these roles can provide greater responsibility and visibility on campus, while at the same time leading to isolation and constraints on access to professional development. This isolation can be amplified on rural campuses where new professionals might lack professional peers.

For college union professionals who move from a large public institution to a small college, the struggle to replicate more specialized programming with limited resources and staffing can be frustrating. Porter Butts (1937/2012) recognized that the role of a college union was often limited by size of the staff supporting it. Butts (1937/2012) stated, "the answer becomes clear that if unions are to do what they want to do and if the directors are to lead reasonably normal lives, the building must be manned by a larger supervisory staff" (p. 58).

The breadth of responsibilities held by a small number of staff members might limit what can be accomplished outside of required work obligations. A challenge for administrators at a small college union is finding time for scholarly work and publication to help advance effective practices and research about small college experiences and management. This challenge has contributed to the dearth of scholarly work pertaining to college unions at small colleges.

Student Employment and Paraprofessionals

Given the likelihood of a smaller professional staff in most college unions at small colleges, student employees may play a significant role in the day-to-day operations of college union facilities. In this regard, a college union supports the educational mission of a college because students who work in such on-campus roles have been found to be more likely to persist and attain a bachelor's degree within four years, and demonstrate a higher degree of satisfaction with college (Astin, 1993). However, developing a quality program that connects student employment and learning requires time and effort from professional staff (Lewis & Contreras, 2009). Because of the multiple responsibilities juggled by most college union staff, a student employment program at a small school could feature less training, feedback, and assessment than at a larger institution (Reynolds, 2009). Nevertheless, the expanded role for student employees in small college unions requires significant attention to these matters.

In addition to the potential for increased student employee responsibility in small college unions, student roles as paraprofessionals can also be significant. In the absence of professional staff, student leaders on many small college campuses have taken on the responsibility of supporting their peers in planning and executing large events, facilitating workshops, and creating training publications (Floyd et al., 1986). These student jobs offer deeper responsibility, thus creating paraprofessional experiences in small college unions that alleviate staffing pressures for professional staff, while providing rich learning opportunities for students.

Facility Management

Day-to-day operations of college unions at small colleges are more likely to be decentralized and rely heavily on other institutional departments. It is not uncommon for departments who do not report to a college union director to play key roles in maintaining the facility, securing it, and possibly overseeing the contracts of service providers, such as dining, mail service, or a bookstore. While this decentralized approach to managing the college union removes some responsibility from the professionals working in the college union, it increases the need for clear and intentional communication and coordination.

Budgets and Finance

Although most student affairs units at small colleges are funded by tuition and fees (Heida, 2006), the financial operations for college unions at small colleges vary as much as their physical space. Some college unions can operate as partial auxiliary services, deriving revenue through food service, conference services, and possible bookstore management. However, the small size of the college community and the degree to which the college union can serve the needs of the broader community mean that college unions at small colleges are not likely to be financially self-sufficient (Heida, 2006). As such, these college unions are typically heavily dependent on tuition and enrollment. During periods of enrollment stability or prosperity, professionals at small college unions are better positioned to meet programming and facility needs while a seemingly small decline in enrollment can significantly impact budgetary resources.

Small College Programming

While the importance of providing community programming is no less important for college unions at small colleges, the space and resources available can significantly affect campus events. Campus programming can be significantly influenced by a college's mission, population, location, and identity. Leishman and Messenger (2010) described a number of trends for programming in college unions at small colleges, including the popularity of late-night programming, leadership programming, and finals week programming. It is unlikely, however, that college union programming at a small college would enjoy the same economy of scale that would allow larger public institutions to produce frequent large-scale events.

Campuses in proximity to other institutions could form partnerships for programs and facility use. Columbia College Chicago, faced with limited space in downtown Chicago, collaborated with nearby Roosevelt University to share Roosevelt's fitness center. In exchange for Columbia students using the space, Columbia funded a full-time personal trainer to work in the facility and provide services for both Columbia and Roosevelt students. Through this partnership, both institutions provided resources to their students that neither could support individually (Weber, 2013).

The Future of Small College Unions

Many significant pressures face small colleges and, ultimately, the college unions housed at these institutions. Since the mid-1980s, scholars have forecasted that shifting demographics, economic pressures, and technological innovative would force small colleges, and their significant components, such as the college union, to radically evolve (Kuh & McAleenan, 1986). A recent article in *The Economist* described the growing economic consensus that "the higher education bubble" would burst soon (The Economist, 2012). While this chorus of bleak forecasts varies from modest to extreme, writers from *The Economist* observe that for smaller colleges who lack big endowments cuts will be significant. Given that in most instances the college union at small colleges is heavily reliant on tuition and fees, these cuts could significantly impact already small budgets.

The second perceived horseman of the apocalypse for higher education is technology, which is not only making scholarly content available to the masses with increasing frequency (Kolowich, 2013) but also provides opportunities as discussed in Chapter 6. The growing industry of online delivery of educational credits will force small college administrators and faculty to rethink how, when, and where students want to learn. Future demand for higher education may not include a traditional campus and the attendant costs associated with a physical facility.

Despite the challenges, it is clear that the role of college unions at small colleges will remain vital. Over the past decade, many reformers have reported that the future of higher education called for a re-envisioning of the landscape of higher education, which removes barriers between the academic and cocurricular, and which recognizes that students' every interaction with campus can be educational (Keeling, 2004). As described in

Learning Reconsidered: A Campus-Wide Focus on the Student Experience, this seamless context for learning, which places the student as an active agent in their own learning and development, has been the role of college unions since their inception (Keeling, 2004). Given the expanded responsibility students at small colleges have in creating community, the strong sense in which institutional mission informs students' interaction with the college union, and the increased likelihood for student interaction with faculty and administrators, college unions at small colleges will remain crucially important as higher education evolves.

Ultimately, regardless of physical size or staff organization, college unions located at small colleges are special places. Many long-time student affairs staff at small colleges recognize that small colleges have a unique culture (Oblander, 2006) and a real community, or a family (Goffigon et al., 1986), which requires a special type of individual. Students at a small school are more likely to know one another and have one or multiple connections to faculty and staff outside of the classroom (Goffigon et al., 1986). Paul Kluge (1993) echoed this sentiment of specialness and community in his classic *Alma Mater: A College Homecoming*. He explains this special connection:

> It's remarkable how people remember their first sight of the god-blessed, god-forsaken college, their tales of driving through town and missing the pace entirely ... some begrudge every mile they travel, others love arriving in a far-off, small place. The two groups: the passers-through and the stayers-on, the ones who say, "Oh, my," and the others who pronounce "Oh, shit!" (p. 19)

For the authors, the relationship-based environment of a small college was the best and most appropriate environment for their undergraduate education and, subsequently, their careers as student affairs professionals.

References

Association of College Unions International (ACUI). (1996). *The role of the college union.* Bloomington, IN: Author.

Association of College Unions International (ACUI). (2008). *Union spotlight: St. Norbert College.* Retrieved from http://www.acui.org/publications/bulletin/article .aspx?issue=702&id=7460

Association of College Unions International (ACUI). (2012). *Small school community of practice.* Retrieved from http://www.acui.org/groups/group.aspx?id=4192

Astin, A. (1993). *What matters in college? Four critical years revisited.* San Francisco, CA: Jossey-Bass.

Bourassa, M. (2012). *How the role of Marbeck Center at Bluffton University came to life.* Retrieved from http://www.acui.org/commons/index .aspx?blogid=25838&id=18276

Butts, P. (1937/2012). Administratively, it's not a one-man job. In P. Butts, E. Beltramini, M. Bourassa, P. Connelly, R. Meyer, S. Mitchell, J. Smith, & T. J. Willis (Eds.), *The college union idea* (2nd ed., p. 58). Bloomington, IN: Association of College Unions International.

Butts, P. (1971). *The college union idea.* Stanford, CA: Association of College Unions International.

Carnegie Foundation for the Advancement of Teaching (Carnegie). (2012). *Classification description.* Retrieved from http://classifications.carnegiefoundation.org/descriptions/size_setting.php

Council for the Advancement of Standards (CAS). (2009). *Higher education self-assessment guide for college unions.* Washington, DC: Author.

Cumberland, W. (1991). *History of Buena Vista College.* Ames: Iowa State Press.

Cutright, M. J. (1995). *An ever-widening circle: The Elmhurst College years.* Elmhurst, IL: Elmhurst College Press.

Davidson College. (2012). *Inside Knobloch Campus Center.* Retrieved from http://www2.davidson.edu/studentlife/inside/IN_main.asp

The Economist. (2012, August 4). *The college-cost calamity.* Retrieved from http://www.economist.com/node/21559936

Fain, P. (2005, September 9). Is less more at small colleges? *The Chronicle of Higher Education.* Retrieved from http://chronicle.com/article/Is-Less-More-at-Small/24054

Floyd, D., Hendricks, W., Larson, S., Mabey, C., McAleenan, A., Mattson, R., . . . Rood, R. (1986). Innovative programming: The small college approach. In G. D. Kuh & A. C. McAleenan (Eds.), *Private dreams, shared visions: Student affairs work in small colleges* (pp. 57–58). Washington, DC: National Association of Student Personnel Administrators.

Goffigon, R., Lacey, D., Wright, J., & Kuh, G. (1986). The small college experience: The generalist's perspective. In G. D. Kuh & A. C. McAleenan (Eds.), *Private dreams, shared visions: Student affairs work in small colleges* (pp. 95–104). Washington, DC: National Association of Student Personnel Administrators.

Heida, D. E. (2006). The student affairs portfolio in small colleges. In S. B. Westfall (Ed.), *New Directions for Student Services: No. 116. The small college dean* (pp. 15–29). San Francisco, CA: Jossey-Bass.

Hoover, E. (2005, November 25). Can small colleges survive? *The Chronicle of Higher Education.* Retrieved from http://chronicle.com/article/Can-Small-Colleges-Survive-/20978

Keeling, R. P. (Ed.). (2004). *Learning reconsidered: A campus-wide focus on the student experience.* Washington, DC: ACPA/NASPA.

Kluge, P. F. (1993). *Alma mater: A college homecoming.* Reading, MA: Addison-Wesley.

Kolowich, S. (2013, May 30). In deals with 10 public universities, Coursera bids for role in credit courses. *The Chronicle of Higher Education.* Retrieved from http://chronicle.com/article/In-Deals-With-10-Public/139533/

Kuh, G., & McAleenan, A. C. (Eds.). (1986). *Private dreams, shared visions: Student affairs work in small colleges.* Washington, DC: National Association of Student Personnel Administrators.

Leishman, K., & Messenger, R. (2010). Programming at small schools: Trends in late-night, leadership, and finals week activities. *The Bulletin of the Association of College Unions International, 78*(6). Retrieved from http://www.acui.org/publications/bulletin/article.aspx?issue=22645&id=13820

Lewis, J., & Contreras, S. (2009). Student learning outcomes: Empirical research as the bridge between theory and practice. In B. Perozzi (Ed.), *Enhancing student learning through college employment.* Bloomington, IN: Association of College Unions International.

McDonald, W. M., & Associates. (Eds.). (2002). *Creating campus community: In search of Ernest Boyer's legacy*. San Francisco, CA: Jossey-Bass.

National Association of College and University Business Officers (NACUBO). (2013). *Small institutions*. Retrieved from http://www.nacubo.org/Membership _and_Community/Small_Institutions-x8440.html

National Orientation Directors Association (NODA). (2013). *Small college network*. Retrieved from https://noda.site-ym.com/?page=network_small

North Park University. (2013). *The time is now: The Johnson Center*. Retrieved from http://www.northpark.edu/Giving/Campaign/Stories/The-Time-is-Now.aspx

Oblander, D. O. (2006). Student affairs staffing in the small college. In S. B. Westfall (Ed.), *New Directions for Student Services: No. 116. The small college dean* (pp. 31–44). San Francisco, CA: Jossey-Bass.

Reynolds, Z. P. (2009). Administrative aspects of student employment. In B. Perozzi (Ed.), *Enhancing student learning through college employment* (pp. 163–164). Bloomington, IN: Association of College Unions International.

Ripon College. (2013). *Ripon College buildings*. Retrieved from http://www .ripon.edu/library/archives/building-guide

Roosevelt University. (2013). *A vertical campus*. Retrieved from http://www.roosevelt.edu/CampusCommunity/Wabash.aspx

Strietelmeier, J. (1959). *Valparaiso's first century*. Valparaiso, IN: Valparaiso University.

Weber, A. (2013, September 16). Columbia, Roosevelt work out gym dean. *The Columbia Chronicle*, p. 1.

Westfall, S. B. (2006a). Charting the territory. In S. B. Westfall (Ed.), *New Directions for Student Services: No. 116. The small college dean* (pp. 5–13). San Francisco, CA: Jossey-Bass.

Westfall, S. B. (Ed.). (2006b). *New Directions for Student Services: No. 116. The small college dean*. San Francisco, CA: Jossey-Bass.

IAN CRONE *is the associate dean of students and director of the Frick Center at Elmhurst College.*

ERIC TAMMES *is the assistant vice president for student communication and marketing at Roosevelt University.*

8

This chapter provides a global perspective on today's college unions.

Globalization and College Unions

Tamara Yakaboski, Brett Perozzi

In 1967, Porter Butts critiqued that "we in the United States had looked inward too much, too long, and that perhaps we could understand our own [college] union development better… if we learned more…about the directions the union idea was taking in other countries" (p. viii). Knowledge about internationalizing college unions or about models in other countries has not progressed significantly in the last 45 years yet international student mobility and internationalization of higher education both have increased substantially (Knight, 2013).

As of 2007, there were more than 150 million students enrolled in higher education globally resulting in 26% of college-aged individuals enrolled in higher education (Altbach, Reisberg, & Rumbley, 2009) and this number is projected to grow exponentially to 262 million by 2025 (Maslen, 2012). The United States attracts a significant number of international students that make up 3.5% of the total U.S. student population (Institute of International Education [IIE], 2011) with that number only expected to increase (Maslen, 2012). China and India provide the largest percentage of students and many higher education institutions are reaching out to recruit from a variety of countries especially Middle Eastern and Asian nations (IIE, 2011; McMurtrie, 2011).

The competition for full-fee-paying international students has become big business and countries are doing their best to be attractive destinations for foreign students. For example, in 2010–2011, the United Kingdom enrolled 480,755 with the same top two countries of origin followed by U.S., German, and Nigerian students (Institute of International Education, n.d.). Europe has taken a lead role in encouraging the global development of its students with the Bologna process and the Erasmus scheme, which has linked an entire region of the world and set the stage for massive student mobility (Teichler, 2012). Major changes in both immigration and tuition fee policies in countries such as the United Kingdom, Australia, and The Netherlands have challenged conventional ideologies. China and India are moving rapidly to accommodate their populations, with no shortage of infrastructure and capacity dilemmas, along with working to send students

NEW DIRECTIONS FOR STUDENT SERVICES, no. 145, Spring 2014 © 2014 Wiley Periodicals, Inc.
Published online in Wiley Online Library (wileyonlinelibrary.com) • DOI: 10.1002/ss.20082

abroad for education, particularly at the graduate level. The Middle East and Southeast Asian countries continue to position themselves as major education hubs, in part by partnering with more established higher education partners such as the United States and Australia. South America, particularly Brazil, is moving rapidly to educate their citizens, whether in-country or abroad.

Given these growing trends, it is important for college union professionals to be globally competent by serving international students and learning from global colleagues. The common approach for many student affairs and services professionals[1] and faculty is to rely on a campus international education center to provide essential support services and programs. A growing concern with this model is that these professionals are often overworked with too few staff members and processing complex visa issues (Lee, 2008), and thereby campuses fail to offer additional educational programs and services that target international students (Kher, Juneau, & Molstad, 2003). College unions can partner with the international office and other international groups to create a more inclusive community through programmatic and educational endeavors.

Higher education staff and faculty need to be proactive in serving international students as they often face issues of discrimination (Jon, 2012; Lee & Rice, 2007; Neider, 2011), loneliness, and difficulty forming relationships (Sawir, Marginson, Deumert, Nyland, & Ramia, 2008), yet can experience personal development from positive engagement with domestic students (Hanassab & Tidwell, 2002). While needs, experiences, and services generally differ between domestic and international students, the educational role college unions can play may transcend borders between these groups. One critical element of college unions' educational missions is to help domestic students become globally competent citizens, which can be accomplished through internationalizing college unions' services and programs but also through designing meaningful interactions and encouraging relationships with international students. Porter Butts's (1967) call for increased global awareness is even more relevant to today's college union professional and they must move college unions' concept to one that promotes global engagement, provides services for a changing global population, and designs spaces inclusive of the global community.

Globalization and Internationalization of Higher Education

Globalization and internationalization have encouraged growth in access to higher education, the mobility and migration of students worldwide, internationalization of curriculum, and the global nature of the educational marketplace. Globalization is "the flow of technology, economy, knowledge, people, values, and ideas... across borders" (Knight, 2008, p. 208). While, internationalization is a result of globalization and the "process of fostering intentional, multidimensional, and interdisciplinary leadership-driven

NEW DIRECTIONS FOR STUDENT SERVICES • DOI: 10.1002/ss

activities that expand global learning, for example, knowledge, skills, and attitudes" (Osfield & Terrell, 2009, p. 121). Douglass, King, and Feller (2009) labeled higher education as globalization's muse, because of how well it lends itself as a platform for the amelioration of global issues, such as creative thinking, talent development, and scientific discovery.

College unions are in a position on campuses to embrace the internationalization of higher education. As the living room and hearthstone of the campus (Butts, 1971), college unions are uniquely poised to embrace international concepts in overt ways through intentional programming, physical representations (e.g., paintings, sculpture, flags), and targeted outreach to international students. These efforts can help students feel connected to campus and assist them with their learning and development. Globalization, internationalization, and the associated mobility of today's college students necessitate that colleges and universities think differently and more broadly about their work with students, especially as it relates to connections among campus entities and surrounding the surrounding community (Torres & Walbert, 2010). College unions often are organized as part of student affairs divisions, which means that college union professionals need to understand their larger role in serving students across multiple areas and supporting the internationalization of campus and the global development of students.

Student Engagement and the Role of College Unions

Given current global economic conditions and population growth, there is a demand from employers for higher education faculty and administrators to prepare students for the global market (Association of American Colleges and Universities [AAC&U], 2010). This provides an opportunity for professionals in college unions to play an intentional role in engaging students through programming, employment, and leadership opportunities to help them be successful in an international society. According to the Association of American Colleges and Universities (AAC&U, 2013) engaging students globally means that they will embrace "complex, interdependent global systems (natural, physical, social, cultural, political) and their implications and legacies through real-world contexts . . . [and] become informed, empathetic, and responsible citizens who understand and reflect on how their actions impact both local and global communities" (p. 1). Given this broad definition, college unions are positioned to embrace various aspects of the concept, such as creating conditions that mimic real-world contexts and offer time for individual reflection providing students the opportunity to recognize the appropriate skills and knowledge base they have learned and how that will apply in a global environment.

Educating students through programmatic elements might include partnering with faculty members and colleagues in areas such as the international office, residential life, or career services. College unions play a role in setting the tone for a campus culture and reflect the community back to itself. With a reframing of philosophy and approach, college unions can infuse international elements into most services and programs. Intentional and proactive programming has the capacity to impact the campus culture. The types of celebrations, events, and programs provided can further support institutional goals while providing a global perspective on critical issues. Whether staff in a college union are hosting events within the facility, or actively engaged in planning those events, working together with colleagues and partners across the institution is vital. The synergy created by multiple perspectives allows for full exposure to crucial world issues and helps infuse international perspectives into all programming across the cocurriculum.

Robert Gates, former U.S. Secretary of Defense and President of Texas A&M University, stated in an interview with *International Educator* that campuses need to "get these students engaged in campus activities and make them feel a part of the university community and university family" (Loveland, 2012, p. 12). Helping international students feel comfortable at their institution and engaged in their academic experience is paramount to providing a range of programming that appeals to them. Understanding the needs and desires of international students is essential to planning quality, attractive programming. Bowman (2012) spoke to the importance of social networks and meaningful connections with new people and surroundings. Supporting international students with their transition is a role for which college unions are well poised. The types of programming for which college unions are responsible differ greatly due to a number of variables such as country or region, institution type, and student characteristics. Approaching programming from a global perspective provides the community with an awareness of issues that can be embraced by multiple genres such as debates, lectures, fine arts, and recreation. From managing nightclubs to lending laptops, from major concerts to poetry readings, college unions serve a critical role within their communities to provide quality programming that reflects cultural competence and helps prepare students for their role in a global society.

As an employer of students on campus, college unions can leverage this opportunity to help students understand one another and become more globally engaged. Student employment (called "casual" employment in some countries) is conceptualized differently in many countries and implemented in various ways. Since U.S. federal regulations restrict international students from working off-campus (8CFR214.2(f)), college unions have the opportunity to employ a large number of international students. Intentional focus on global learning outcomes in training and job orientation allows college unions to positively impact students' intercultural understanding. Given the increase in reports of discrimination against international students (Glass & Braskamp, 2012), college unions can use this as a point of departure for globally focused educational programming. This may require expanding staff diversity trainings to include topics on biases against international students to prevent discrimination during the hiring phase.

College unions have a long tradition of helping students develop through leadership roles on campus. By focusing on intentionally including international students in these experiences professionals in college unions can help students better understand cultural nuances, global perspectives, and social mores of various cultures. Staff can demonstrate the value of international concepts by developing learning outcomes for leadership experiences and partnering with students on learning assessment. Providing the necessary education and training for students is essential for acquisition of the desired outcomes.

Student Affairs and Professionals in College Unions

Outside of the United States, many professionals doing student affairs work come from academic and other backgrounds rather than a formal curriculum and experience in student affairs. Some may have been, or still are, faculty members, psychological counselors, or even bankers. Those in college union may have been chefs, social workers, or accountants. The United States has graduate education programs in student affairs and higher education administration. Some Canadian institutions offer graduate programs of this type, and many countries such as Australia, China, and the United Arab Emirates provide formalized training for staff. To increase knowledge and skills around global competencies, intercultural understanding, and other learning outcome areas, professional associations offer a variety of educational programs. NASPA, Student Affairs Administrators in Higher Education, provides graduate-credit-bearing study tours (in collaboration with other associations such as ACPA, College Student Educators International), administrative exchanges, published resources, and the annual International Symposium. In 2012, the Association of College Unions International (ACUI) piloted an international job shadowing program for international members to visit and participate in a U.S. college union, and ACUI is a key partner in the collaborative study tours (ACUI, 2012). The Association of College and University Housing Officers International, and several other professional associations offer a number of ways for members to be involved internationally.

Professionals in college unions can become more knowledgeable about international and global issues through a variety of methods. While associations offer a range of programs and services for staff that enrich intercultural understanding, staff can also approach learning from a more personal perspective by learning another language or traveling internationally. This demonstrates a commitment to other cultures and provides an appreciation for communication and diversity. Study abroad travel can also be enlightening and life changing in some circumstances, and helps shape one's worldview and perspective. Finally, interested staff can read about or research other cultures and concepts surrounding intercultural understanding.

Student Affairs and Globalization of College Unions

Student affairs work differs substantially around the world. The U.S. conceptualization of student affairs is focused on tangible measures such as recruitment, retention, persistence, and graduation, as well as student attainment of learning outcomes. Learning outcomes in a North American paradigm typically are established using an institution's general education learning outcomes, borrowed from established sources (such as professional associations), or developed organically by the student affairs division (Perozzi, Kappes, & Santucci, 2009). Outcomes are often the primary focus of a U.S. model, yet providing key services and programs for the campus community are also important, and ideally incorporate international students and global concepts. The extent to which college unions are embedded in a student affairs philosophy will differ, dictating the paradigm and practical implementation of programs and services; in other words, professional college unions may either view themselves as contributing to the development of students or more simply as service providers (Davis, 2011). The cultural context and inherent values surrounding work with students will ultimately guide union staff. The degree to which student affairs as a profession has developed in a country or region will focus the lens for college union professionals in that area.

ACUI uses the term "college union" to describe the various programs and associated facilities that constitute the "union," yet the union is not limited to a physical structure, rather it is the idea and concept coined by Porter Butts (1967, 1971). This conceptualization may not ring true for college union models around the world as they have evolved. An account from 1960 found 279 college union buildings or plans for buildings outside of North America across 49 countries (Butts, 1960). Unfortunately, there is no updated account of overseas college unions in existence today. Overall, college unions seek to create community on campus:

> ...they are one of the only entities in higher education that almost always (across all countries) blend an organizational identity as a 'set of programmes and ideas' together with a physical facility. The organizations provide a sense of place through both ideological contexts in terms of programmes and services that address issues of the day and activities that invite students to engage, while simultaneously using a physical structure to encourage informal dialogue, socialization and community-building activities. (Perozzi & O'Brien, 2009, p. 95)

New Directions for Student Services • DOI: 10.1002/ss

In the United States, terminology varies widely, incorporating such organizational labels as student union, college union, student center, and university center. All of the labels attempt to demonstrate the centrality of the program and facility to the institution, and its primary importance to the campus community. College union buildings may be financed by bonds, often backed by student fees; thus, the word "student" is frequently in the name of the organization and/or building. Ideally, the concept of a college union embodies the culture and unique aspects of an institution, and frequently of the surrounding community, by reinforcing unique and essential cultural elements through physical expressions, programmatic endeavors, and targeted partnerships. As college campuses worldwide have internationalized, communities consist of greater numbers of international students and as such calls for college unions to embrace a global identity and role.

There is no one European model of student affairs, but, generally, the focus is on student mobility, student financial aid, and service provision. For example, established in 1999, the European Council for Student Affairs (ECStA) has worked as an independent organization to increase cooperation between 18 different higher education organizations in 14 countries (ECStA, 2005). They have expanded beyond student mobility to include funding, housing, food services, counseling, cultural programs, and general student services (ECStA, n.d.). In an ECStA (2005) review of European student affairs models, they found there was no one organizational structure. Instead, some countries have a national organization that oversees services for all institutions such as *Centre National des Œuvres Universitaires et Scolaires* (CNOUS) in France or *Associazione Nazionale Organizzazione Diritto allo Studio Universitario* (ANDISU) in Italy. France's CNOUS focuses on student improvement via food, housing, funding, social and cultural activities, and mobility (CNOUS, n.d.). In some countries there are local and regional associations that provide services to college and university students, called CNOUS in France and *Studentenwerke* in Germany, and organized there by the German National Organization for Student Affairs or Deutsches Studentenwerk. Each local *Studentenwerke* allows the individual higher education institution to focus on their essential academic mission, and the local or regional *Studentenwerke* provides services such as accommodation (housing) and catering (dining services) and supports students in their independent quest for higher learning and may provide services such as counseling, health care, and cultural or sporting programming (Schäferbarthold, 1999). Countries like Australia offer a wide range of programs and services and focus most on customer service than on student development or learning outcomes. College unions may or may not exist, and where they do, they may house or provide these functions.

In most European countries, the "student(s) union" is roughly equivalent to U.S. student government but incorporates a sense of autonomy that is only seen in a few U.S. states such as California and Florida

NEW DIRECTIONS FOR STUDENT SERVICES • DOI: 10.1002/ss

(Permaul, Mann, & Perozzi, 2009). For example, the National Union of Students (NUS) in the United Kingdom is an association for individual students' unions in the United Kingdom, and the organization of the same name brings together students' unions across Australia. The European student union governs through their elected leaders and often owns and operates facilities that provide services for students and, to a lesser extent, the broader campus community.

Student unions can be separately incorporated from the institutions where they reside. For example, at Monash University in Australia a separate corporation, Monyx, has been established with its own board of directors and chief executive officer. Monyx is responsible for most student-related functions including the union concept (Perozzi & O'Brien, 2011). This concept has similarities to U.S. California universities and their associated auxiliary services that are governed by student-majority boards (Permaul et al., 2009).

Another example, the Kenyan model, is in transition and began more as the student-run model meant to encourage student leadership and serve as a shared place for student community including services such as concessions, pubs, or computer labs. As internationalization increases, a more entrepreneurial or market model of college unions has emerged that serves as a facility for services and student government offices as well as administrative offices accompanied with a shift of control away from student run (Yakaboski, 2011).

College Union Services for a Global Population

College unions are complex organizations capable of impacting the campus community through their programs, services, and, where relevant, structures. Intentional planning to internationalize services for the campus community can be a way college unions demonstrate global competency and inclusivity. Weaving a global focus through services can help students understand the connectedness between various aspects of their life. For example, most college unions operate or encompass campus dining venues. Global themes can be ameliorated through food: from obtaining recipes from students to allowing them to prepare food in the kitchens, and from simple, educational displays about cuisine to themed days, weeks, or months designed to pair meaningful information with the everyday dining experience. Regularly providing specialty meals, such as those prepared hallal and kosher, demonstrates to international and domestic students alike that they are cared about and that food is an integral aspect of cultural understanding. At Stanford University, the dining hall uses Jewish and Muslim student dining ambassadors to advise the staff on meals and cooking techniques that are aligned with religious traditions (Karlin-Neumann & Sanders, 2013).

New Directions for Student Services • DOI: 10.1002/ss

In addition to dining, college unions can consider their communication plans, the ways in which they reach and attract students, and visual representations within their facilities. College unions can exhibit an accepting institutional culture by having telephone calling cards available on campus (although these are diminishing in popularity as technology advances), and making facilities available for Skyping with family and friends abroad. Moreover, the way in which a college union is decorated can further promote a welcoming environment for all students at the institution. A focus on international art in its many forms helps diversify the visual displays in the union, and featuring a country or countries in some way in the union can help the organization connect with specific students from those areas. For example, the University of Pittsburg asks international students to send pictures of bridges in their countries (a theme in Pittsburg because of their many bridges) and then the pictures are enlarged and displayed in the union during the first few weeks of the fall semester.

Also, college unions can dedicate space to create clean, inviting, and readily available nondenominational "meditation rooms" that have policies allowing the use of candles and incense. These rooms have become increasingly widespread in college unions and are popular among international students, especially those of Islamic faith who require private or semi-private space for prayer several times a day. For example, Stanford University used a recent renovation of the Old Union to dedicate the third floor to religious engagement and practice through a new Center for Inter-Religious Community, Learning and Experiences (CIRCLE; Karlin-Neumann & Sanders, 2013).

Some university facilities in Australia provide foot-washing stations for their Muslim students in addition to multidenominational rooms for individual and small group use. In the United States providing ritual stations for ablutions has been more challenging to incorporate into college union spaces as redesigning rooms and bathrooms can be costly and space unavailable. Duke University's solution was to provide slip-resistant mats in the bathrooms nearest the center's prayer room and to work with housekeeping staff to increase their cultural sensitivity and understanding of the impact of wet surfaces within college unions (Sapp, 2013).

Conclusion

Globalization and internationalization of the expanding higher education sector have had a significant impact on the student affairs profession and the role college unions play in providing a venue for international students to engage in the campus community. College unions can impact their campus communities and individual students by serving as a galvanizing entity bringing people together to learn and meaningfully interact. College unions provide safe and inviting environments and/or a context for the college campus; they help set the tone and shape the culture, which can be supportive of global perspectives. A primary role of a college union is to serve gathering places for the campus community, providing symbols and icons that demonstrate an understanding of the multiple cultural backgrounds of individuals within the college or university. With greater ethnic, religious, and political diversity on college campuses, college unions can help pave the way to international learning and understanding. It is past time to update Porter Butts's original works and directories on the overseas college union and to be more intentional about internationalizing staff and student development through cross-border collaborations and global programming.

Note

1. For the purpose of this chapter, the phrase "student affairs" is used as a comprehensive umbrella term that includes student services broadly. Internationally, this work is generally referred to as student services rather than student affairs.

References

Altbach, P. G., Reisberg, L., & Rumbley, L. E. (2009). *Trends in global higher education: Tracking an academic revolution*. UNESCO 2009 World Conference on Higher Education. Paris, France: UNESCO.

Association of American Colleges and Universities (AAC&U). (2010). *Employers seek more college-educated workers with higher level of learning and broader sets of skills, new survey reveals*. Retrieved from http://www.aacu.org/press_room/press_releases/2010/employersurvey.cfm

Association of American Colleges and Universities (AAC&U). (2013, February 18). *Global learning VALUE rubric*. Paper presented at the Association of International Education Administrators conference, New Orleans, LA.

Association of College Unions International (ACUI). (2012, September). International delegates complete job shadowing program pilot. *The Bulletin, 80*(5). Retrieved from http://www.acui.org/publications/bulletin/article.aspx?issue=36082&id=18862

Bowman, K. D. (2012). Local connections: Helping international students find a welcoming place within the local community. *International Educator*, Nov./Dec., 27–33.

Butts, P. (1960). Overseas unions. In C. A. Berry & A. R. Looman (Eds.), *College unions...year fifty* (pp. 191–198). Ithaca, NY: Association of College Unions.

Butts, P. (1967). *State of college unions around the world*. Ithaca, NY: Association of College Unions International.

Butts, P. (1971). *College unions idea*. Stanford, CA: Association of College Unions International.

Centre National des Œuvres Universitaires et Scolaires (CNOUS). (n.d.). *About us*. Retrieved from http://www.cnous.fr/index.php?lg=fr&refresh=1

Davis, T. (2011). In this age of consumerism, what are the implications of giving students what they want? Have it your way U. In P. M. Magolda & M. B. Baxter Magolda (Eds.), *Contested issues in student affairs: Diverse perspectives and respectful dialogue* (pp. 85–102). Sterling, VA: Stylus.

Douglass, J. A., King, C. J., & Feller, I. (Eds.). (2009). *Globalization's muse: Universities and higher education systems in a changing world*. Berkeley: University of California Press.

European Council for Student Affairs (ECStA). (n.d.). *About us*. Retrieved from http://www.ecsta.org/en

European Council for Student Affairs (ECStA). (2005). Comparison of the student service organizations in Europe. *ECStA Report*. Retrieved from http://www.ecsta .org/assets/8/ECStA_2005_Report_Comparison_of_the_Student_Service_Organisations _in_Europe.pdf

Glass, C. R., & Braskamp, L. A. (2012, October 26). Essay on how colleges should respond to racism against international students. *Inside Higher Ed*. Retrieved from http://www.insidehighered.com/views/2012/10/26/essay-how-colleges-should-respond -racism-against-international-students

Hanassab, S., & Tidwell, R. (2002). International students in higher education: identification of needs and implications for policy and practice. *Journal of Studies in International Education, 6*, 305–322.

Institute of International Education. (2011). Top 25 places of origin of international scholars, 2009/10-2010/11. *Open Doors Report on International Educational Exchange*. Retrieved from http://www.iie.org/en/Research-and-Publications/Open -Doors/Data/International-Students/Leading-Places-of-Origin/2009-11

Institute of International Education. (n.d.). International students in the United Kingdom, 2010/2011. *Project Atlas*. Retrieved from http://www.iie.org/en/Services /Project-Atlas/United-Kingdom/International-Students-In-UK

Jon, J. E. (2012). Power dynamics with international students: From the perspective of domestic students in Korean higher education. *Higher Education, 64*(4), 441–454.

Karlin-Neumann, P., & Sanders, J. (2013). Bringing faith to campus: Religious and spiritual space, time, and practice at Stanford University. *Journal of College & Character, 14*(2), 125–132.

Kher, N., Juneau, G., & Molstad, S. (2003). From the southern hemisphere to the rural south: A Mauritian students' version of "Coming to America." *College Student Journal, 37*(4), 564–569.

Knight, J. (2008). Internationalization: Concepts, complexities and challenges. In J. F. Forest & P. G. Altbach (Eds.), *International handbook of higher education* (pp. 207– 228). Dordrecht, The Netherlands: Springer.

Knight, J. (2013). From multi-national universities to education hubs to eduglomerates? *IIE Networker*, p. 42.

Lee, J. J. (2008). Beyond borders: International student pathways to the U.S. *Journal of Studies in International Education, 12*(3), 308–327.

Lee, J. J., & Rice, C. (2007). Welcome to America? International student perceptions of discrimination. *Higher Education, 53*(3), 381–409.

Loveland, E. (2012). International education and national security: Interview with Robert M. Gates. *International Educator*, Nov./Dec., 10–12.

Maslen, G. (2012, October 19). Worldwide student numbers forecast to double by 2025. *University World News*. Retrieved from http://www.universityworldnews.com/article.php?story=20120216105739999

McMurtrie, B. (2011, November 14). International enrollments at U.S. colleges grow but still rely on China. *The Chronicle of Higher Education*. Retrieved from http://chronicle.com/article/International-Enrollments-at/129747/

Neider, X. N. (2011). "When you come here, it is still like it is their space": Exploring the experiences of students of Middle Eastern heritages in post-9/11 U.S. higher education. *Journal of International Education & Leadership, 1*(1). Retrieved from http://www.jielusa.org/wp-content/uploads/2012 /01/Formatted-Experiences-of-ME-Students_Neider1.pdf

Osfield, K. J., & Terrell, P. S. (2009). Internationalization in higher education and student affairs. In G. S. McClellan & J. Stringer (Eds.), *The handbook of student affairs administration in higher education* (pp. 120–143). San Francisco, CA: Jossey-Bass.

Permaul, N., Mann, J., & Perozzi, B. (2009). When students are in charge. In B. Perozzi (Ed.), *Enhancing student learning through college employment*. Bloomington, IN: Association of College Unions International.

Perozzi, B., Kappes, J., & Santucci, D. (2009). Learning outcomes and student employment programs. In B. Perozzi (Ed.), *Enhancing student learning through college employment*. Bloomington, IN: Association of College Unions International.

Perozzi, B., & O'Brien, A. (2009). College unions/university centres/student centres. In R. Ludeman, K. Osfield, E. Iglesias Hidalgo, D. Oste, & H. S. Wang (Eds.), *Student affairs and services in higher education: Global foundations, issues, and best practices* (2nd ed., pp. 94–96). Paris, France: UNESCO.

Perozzi, B., & O'Brien, A. (2011). The global practice of student affairs: A United States and Australian case study. *Journal of the Australia and New Zealand Student Services Association, 36*, 1–25.

Sapp, C. L. (2013). A great and towering compromise: Religious practice and space at Duke University. *Journal of College & Character, 14*(2), 117–124.

Sawir, E., Marginson, S., Deumert, A., Nyland, C., & Ramia, G. (2008). Loneliness and international students: An Australian study. *Journal of Studies in International Education, 12*(2), 148–180.

Schäferbarthold, D. (1999). The place of student services in German universities. In J. Dalton (Ed.), *New Directions for Student Services: No. 86. Beyond borders: How international developments are changing student affairs practice* (pp. 33–38). San Francisco, CA: Jossey-Bass.

Teichler, U. (2012). International student mobility in Europe in the context of the Bologna process. *Journal of International Education & Leadership, 2*(1). Retrieved from http://www.jielusa.org/wp-content/uploads/2012/01/International-Student-Mobility-in-Europe-in-the-Context-of-the-Bologna-Process1.pdf

Torres, V., & Walbert, J. (2010). Envisioning the future of student affairs. *Final Report of the Task Force on the Future of Student Affairs*. Appointed jointly by ACPA and NASPA.

Yakaboski, T. (2011). Student centers in Kenya: A shift from living rooms to business offices. *ACUI Bulletin, 79*(3), 26–32.

TAMARA YAKABOSKI *is an associate professor in Higher Education and Student Affairs Leadership at the University of Northern Colorado.*

BRETT PEROZZI *is the associate vice president for Student Affairs at Weber State University and the chair of the International Advisory Board for NASPA-Student Affairs Administrators in Higher Education.*

9

This chapter calls for more intentional use and design of assessment, evaluation, and research about the topics and trends in colleges unions highlighted in this volume.

Preparing College Unions for the Future Through Assessment, Evaluation, and Research

Danielle M. De Sawal, Tamara Yakaboski

The assessment movement has been embraced gradually since the 1970s by many student affairs and higher education administrators, a trend that corresponds to increased attention to accountability and public dissatisfaction with the outcomes associated with higher education (Upcraft & Schuh, 1996). Over the last couple of decades higher education administrators have driven the assessment movement, although improving practice based on assessment results can be difficult (Banta & Blaich, 2011).

Professionals working in college unions need to embrace this movement for survival in a climate of declining resources and increased demand for outcomes-based assessment. Without assessment, evaluation, and research, professionals in college unions will not have sufficient evidence to make arguments regarding the importance of student learning and engagement that occurs within these facilities.

To further complicate this challenge, the meanings of assessment, evaluation, and research often are blurred. As Blimling (2001) observed, "If scholarship and practice in student affairs sometimes seem segmented, confused, and conflicted, the reason may be that they are" (p. 381). Part of this segmentation comes from the challenge of connecting results of research and scholarship to day-to-day practice. Specific challenges include lack of knowledge about how to find and incorporate research into observable trends and experiences.

Assessment means to "gather, analyze, and interpret evidence which describes . . . effectiveness" (Stage & Manning, 2003, p. 5) and typically has only implications for the institution in which the assessment is conducted (Upcraft & Schuh, 1996). Effectiveness may include assessing student learning outcomes but, more commonly for professionals in college unions, it is assessing clientele satisfaction and cost-effectiveness.

New Directions for Student Services, no. 145, Spring 2014 © 2014 Wiley Periodicals, Inc.
Published online in Wiley Online Library (wileyonlinelibrary.com) • DOI: 10.1002/ss.20083

Evaluations "use assessment evidence to improve ... effectiveness" (Stage & Manning, 2003, p. 5). Faculty tend to approach research, on the other hand, as "gathering information you need to answer a question" with implications for the larger field of study (Stage & Manning, 2003, p. 5). Although the terms assessment and evaluation can be used interchangeably, Astin and Antonio (2012) highlighted that terminology is important when looking at assessment results. Using terms such as "feedback and assessment results are much less loaded and less threatening than terms such as testing and evaluation" (p. 159).

Assessment, evaluation, and research to improve effectiveness should be a part of a professional's role in a college union. This call for inquiry-based practice aligns with publications such as ACPA's *ASK Standards* (ACPA–College Student Educators International, 2006), which identified assessment approaches, including outcomes-based assessment, as the responsibility of each professional within an institution's division of student affairs.

Creating a Culture of Assessment, Evaluation, and Research

As an integral part of the campus community, professionals in college unions need to consider how to collect, interpret, and present data that support the college union idea (Butts, 1971), which is still a guiding principle for those working in college unions. Throughout this *New Directions for Student Services* edition the authors have identified that the future of college unions will require an examination of how the work of professionals in college unions aligns with the academic and institutional mission. The institutional mission "establishes the tone of a college and conveys its educational purposes" (Kuh, Kinzie, Schuh, Whitt, & Associates, 2005, p. 25). In many cases, the academic mission of the institution clearly articulates the dissemination and creation of knowledge. Professionals need to begin with understanding both the espoused (what is written in the mission statement) and the enacted (what the institution actually does) mission of their own institution (Kuh et al., 2005). Presenting evidence that aligns the programs and services offered in college unions to the academic mission highlights data that will support the current and future expansion of this area of practice.

Student affairs handbooks focus on the role of assessment and evaluation in a professional's daily role (Bresciani, 2011). This focus is aligned with an increase in public demand for accountability and has consistently been presented in the assessment literature for the last few decades (Bresciani, 2011), which results in an understanding by many institutions that assessment is here to stay as part of the future of student affairs. As a result, the focus of professional jobs within the field represents the need for professionals to have skills and knowledge in this area. Hoffman and Bresciani (2010) found that "one in four (27.1%) of the positions posted to *The Placement*

Exchange in 2008 required applicants either to demonstrate competency in assessing student learning or to complete learning assessment duties as a part of the job" (p. 508). As professionals in college unions reorganize and establish priorities for their organizations, consideration should be given to the inclusion of assessment, evaluation, and research skills within their organizations' job descriptions. It should be noted that the establishment of a single position that focuses on student learning and outcomes can provide centralized coordination; however, the focus of the profession is emphasizing that all members of the field need to be versed in the knowledge and skills associated with assessment and evaluation. This emphasis is evidenced in the *ACPA and NASPA Professional Competency Areas for Student Affairs Practitioners* (ACPA/NASPA, 2010) report that highlighted assessment, evaluation, and research as one of the ten competency areas necessary for professionals.

The role of research within the daily lives of college union professionals is not as clearly addressed in the larger body of literature surrounding student affairs practice. Research about the profession is often deferred to the faculty in higher education and student affairs administration programs. College unions provide an environment that has the potential to engage students, connect them to the institution in meaningful ways, and provide the campus community with a common gathering space. A large portion of research is based on large college student samples that provide little direction toward how different types of students benefit or do not from specific experiences (Pascarella & Terenzini, 1991, 2005). College union professionals need to identify where they see gaps in the literature related to the programs and services they offer day-to-day. De Sawal and Yakaboski (2013) identified some gaps within college union fields based on dissertations written over the last 30 years about college unions. An identification of these and other college union areas that need to be explored will provide scholars with ideas for future research studies.

Considerations for Future Assessment, Evaluation, and Research

The current state of college unions reveals that the environment is rich for research. At the same time, it is also clear that if future research is not conducted within this functional area, professionals in college unions will struggle to find evidence in the literature to support and guide their programs and services. Banta, Jones, and Black (2009) called for building a culture based on evidence when looking at designing effective assessment. The existence of effective assessment will be hard to create without a foundation of research that identifies and supports the development or continued existence of programs and services specifically tied to college union organization.

NEW DIRECTIONS FOR STUDENT SERVICES • DOI: 10.1002/ss

The following areas that were highlighted in this volume provide an initial starting place for scholars and practitioners eager to engage in research focused on college unions. These areas also represent those aspects of college union professionals' work that should be included in the assessment and evaluation of their organization.

Student Engagement.   Although a broad topic in student affairs, how college unions specifically contribute to student engagement on campus should be examined. The enacted mission of the institution has been identified as key to understanding student success, since it guides the daily decisions of *where* and *how* students will interact on campus (Kuh et al., 2005). College campuses may or may not have a physical structure such as a dedicated college union facility in which to create these interactions, therefore it becomes even more critical to focus on the intentional ways in which students engage with programs and services offered by college union professionals. Some areas to consider are as follows:

- The role of the college union governing or programming board in creating conditions that enhance student engagement.
- The impact of student employment within the college union as contributing to desired student learning outcomes.
- The role of university wide assessment data on student engagement impacts the programs and services offered in college unions.

Diversity.   Research that examines the experiences of diverse populations in college unions is warranted to help better understand how to most effectively support integration into college, individual development, and how it could contribute to increasing levels of involvement. Specific research is needed to identify how programming for diverse populations may affect the learning environment for students outside of the classroom. Additionally, research that focuses on how technology intersects with programming and the extent to which technology may impede or facilitate meaningful cross-cultural dialogue among our students would be worthwhile. Torres (2010) made the case that looking at learning experiences through the lens of underrepresented populations provides the opportunity to use assessment data to "evaluate how to serve diverse populations and find ways to help all members of the institutional community succeed—not just the few who have always succeeded" (p. 69). Some areas to consider are as follows:

- The impact of multicultural and diversity programming done within college union facilities on student learning outcomes and increasing cultural sensitivity and awareness.
- The representation, recruitment, and retention of underrepresented populations as college union professionals.

- How the college union's organizational structures, policies, mission statements, facility design, and culture encourage and support inclusivity and diversity.

Facility Design and Community.   Historically, college unions represent one of the first facilities on campus to create community outside the academic classroom and dormitories. These facilities provided the ideal context for the academic community to gather for both academic discourse and social events. Today, campuses are building more of these spaces throughout the campus community. College union professionals are faced with a number of considerations related to how to market their facilities and determine what services (e.g., retail, classroom space, offices) should be included within the scope of their operations. Some areas to consider are as follows:

- Explore the impact associated with sustainability construction and operations on the college union's bottom line.
- How physical structures and virtually designed spaces create community, encourage a sense of belonging, and support student learning outcomes.
- The role of college unions in a time when community building is no longer limited to one space but extends across campus and digitally to include academic and student affairs areas.

Fundraising.   As an emerging area within the field, the role of development, fundraising, and philanthropy offer the opportunity to identify not only best practices but also to utilize the college union as a learning laboratory for how to establish giving patterns with the multiple constituencies that are being served. Professionals in college unions will need to understand how to cultivate donors and provide stewardship to those that give. Former student employees and student leaders cannot be the only focus for establishing a donor base. College union staff and others connected with the union will need to share their stories with corporations and community members who also see value in continuing to grow college unions as the gathering place on campus. Some areas to consider are as follows:

- Explore how alumni describe their connections to the college union environments once they have left the institution to better develop stewardship programs and increase alumni giving.
- Examine if connections exist between involvement and/or employment in the college union and giving to the institution.
- The role of special events (e.g., weddings, anniversaries, family reunions) in establishing future donors.

Technology.   The role of technology within college unions will continue to expand as new tools are developed to improve meeting management operations, market programs and services, and enhance student learning initiatives. Professionals in college unions will need to consider how technology shapes their daily interactions with students. Communication with students and community stakeholders continues to shift to more electronic media rather than print materials. Establishing user-friendly interfaces that allow the campus community to be aware of what the college union has to offer will be essential in the future. Professionals have observed technology change faster than they are able to implement new systems on campus. As a result, the purchase and/or use of technology tools within a college union need to be researched as well as how they will impact professionals and students considered. Some areas to consider are as follows:

- Use of technology and social media in college unions for information sharing, marketing, and assessment and evaluation.
- Examine the "shelf-life" of meeting management software systems or other administrative systems that are designed to improve efficiency within college union operations.
- How social media can be used to create community, improve student engagement and involvement, and help students and professionals form academic connections beyond the physical structure of the college union building.

Small College Unions.   Literature surrounding the role of college unions at small colleges is limited. This is an area of research that is ripe for understanding how small colleges create community on campus. Small colleges throughout the United States are inclusive of many different institutional types (e.g., religious, two-year, four-year, ethnic specific) and as a result provide the opportunity to study many different campus cultures. Student affairs professionals at small colleges often work in decentralized administrative environments taking on multiple roles that blur the lines between functional areas in the field. Understanding how these environments function in relation to space usage and staffing practices would fill a gap in the literature about college unions. Some areas to consider are as follows:

- Professional development for small college union staff and the impact of culture on professional satisfaction and job retention.
- Explore how small colleges support the college union ideal by creating community and student engagement without a designated facility or gathering spaces on campus.
- How the role of college unions supports the academic and institutional mission of community colleges.

Globalization and College Unions.   Globalization and internationalization have had profound impacts on higher education worldwide that have trickled down to influence student affairs and college unions. U.S. professionals need to learn from and connect with colleagues across the globe to share best practices but more importantly to learn from their models and student cultures. With the increased mobility of students to and from countries and institutions, college union professionals need to assess how their facilities, programs, and services reflect a global clientele and how they can create more inclusive and welcoming spaces for this increased diversity. This is an area ripe for assessment, evaluation, and research since so little has been written about college unions internationalizing or about college unions worldwide. Some areas to consider are as follows:

- The inclusion of international students in diversity programming and social media usage to support global understanding with domestic students.
- U.S. professional development to focus on collaboration with other student affairs professionals and faculty both in the United States and internationally to bridge the gap on international students and the role of college unions.
- Designing student engagement and involvement through a global paradigm that are supported by college unions.

Charting a Future Through Partnerships With Graduate Preparation Programs

Research specifically related to college unions is limited (Yakaboski, 2012) even though other student affairs functional areas have a foundation of research studies that examine the impact of their specific role on campus (e.g., Greek Life, Residence Life, First Year Experience). Areas of focus that are connected to college unions are being examined in larger contexts (e.g., student engagement, student programming, auxiliary services, higher education fiscal management, multicultural competences, technology, etc.) but provide no direct links to the college union idea. Research focused on college unions will require a partnership with the academic community.

Graduate programs in higher education and student affairs provide the ideal context to engage and encourage research on college unions. A limited number of master's theses and doctoral dissertations in the last 30 years have specifically addressed college unions, with only 23 being identified (Yakaboski & De Sawal, 2013). While college unions across the United States employ graduate students in assistantships, those students do not seem to be identifying the gaps in the literature related to their own work and researching those topics in the classroom. Although college unions are included in many studies, the focus of the study and the findings are examining a trend or issue in higher education from a larger context. College union professionals should actively engage faculty on their campus to present ideas that might be able to be included as suggestions for student research within courses.

New Directions for Student Services • DOI: 10.1002/ss

References

ACPA–College Student Educators International. (2006). *ASK standards*. Washington, DC: Author.

ACPA/NASPA. (2010). *ACPA and NASPA professional competency areas for student affairs practitioners*. Washington, DC: Author.

Astin, A. W., & Antonio, A. L. (2012). *Assessment for excellence: The philosophy and practice of assessment and evaluation in higher education* (2nd ed.). Lanham, MD: Rowman & Littlefield.

Banta, T. W., & Blaich, C. (2011). Closing the assessment loop. *Change*. Retrieved from http://www.changemag.org/Archives/Back%20Issues/2011/January-February%202011/closing-assessment-loop-abstract.html

Banta, T. W., Jones, E. A., & Black, K. E. (2009). *Designing effective assessment: Principles and profiles of good practice*. San Francisco, CA: Jossey-Bass.

Blimling, G. S. (2001). Uniting scholarship and communities of practice in student affairs. *Journal of College Student Development, 42*(4), 381–396.

Bresciani, M. J. (2011). Assessment and evaluation. In J. H. Schuh, S. R. Jones, S. R. Harper, & Associates (Eds.), *Student services: A handbook for the profession* (5th ed., pp. 321–334). San Francisco, CA: Jossey-Bass.

Butts, P. (1971). *College unions idea*. Stanford, CA: Association of College Unions International.

De Sawal, D. M., & Yakaboski, T. (2013). Exploring 30 years of college union dissertations: What we do and don't know. *ACUI Bulletin, 81*(15), 26–31.

Hoffman, J. L., & Bresciani, M. J. (2010). Assessment work: Examining the prevalence and nature of assessment competencies and skills in student affairs job postings. *Journal of Student Affairs Research and Practice, 47*(4), 495–512.

Kuh, G. D., Kinzie, J., Schuh, J. H., Whitt, E. J., & Associates. (2005). *Student success in college: Creating conditions that matter*. San Francisco, CA: Jossey-Bass.

Pascarella, E. T., & Terenzini, P. T. (1991). *How college affects students: Findings and insights from twenty years of research*. San Francisco, CA: Jossey-Bass.

Pascarella, E. T., & Terenzini, P. T. (2005). *How college affects students: A decade of research*. San Francisco, CA: Jossey-Bass.

Stage, F. K., & Manning, K. (2003). *Research in the college context: Approaches and methods*. New York, NY: Brunner-Routledge.

Torres, V. (2010). Assessment and student diversity. In G. L. Kramer & R. L. Swing (Eds.), *Higher education assessments: Leadership matters* (pp. 59–71). New York, NY: Rowman & Littlefield.

Upcraft, M. L., & Schuh, J. H. (1996). *Assessment in student affairs: A guide for practitioners*. San Francisco, CA: Jossey-Bass.

Yakaboski, T. (2012, March). *ACUI's emerging research agenda*. Paper presented at the annual conference of the Association of College Unions International, Boston, MA.

Yakaboski, T., & De Sawal, D. M. (2013, March). *A bold future: 30 years of college union dissertations*. Paper presented at the annual conference of the Association of College Unions International, St. Louis, MO.

Danielle M. De Sawal is a clinical associate professor and coordinator of the Higher Education and Student Affairs master's program at Indiana University.

Tamara Yakaboski is an associate professor in Higher Education and Student Affairs Leadership at the University of Northern Colorado.

Index

Great Resources for Higher Education Professionals

Student Affairs Today

12 issues for $225 (print) / $180 (e)

Get innovative best practices for student affairs plus lawsuit summaries to keep your institution out of legal trouble. It's packed with advice on offering effective services, assessing and funding programs, and meeting legal requirements.

studentaffairstodaynewsletter.com

Campus Legal Advisor

12 issues for $210 (print) / $170 (e)

From complying with the ADA and keeping residence halls safe to protecting the privacy of student information, this monthly publication delivers proven strategies to address the tough legal issues you face on campus.

campuslegaladvisor.com

Campus Security Report

12 issues for $210 (print) / $170 (e)

A publication that helps you effectively manage the challenges in keeping your campus, students, and employees safe. From protecting students on campus after dark to interpreting the latest laws and regulations, *Campus Security Report* has answers you need.

campussecurityreport.com

National Teaching & Learning Forum

6 issues for $65 (print or e)

From big concepts to practical details and from cutting-edge techniques to established wisdom, NTLF is your resource for cross-disciplinary discourse on student learning. With it, you'll gain insights into learning theory, classroom management, lesson planning, scholarly publishing, team teaching, online learning, pedagogical innovation, technology, and more.

ntlf.com

Disability Compliance for Higher Education

12 issues for $230 (print) / $185 (e)

This publication combines interpretation of disability laws with practical implementation strategies to help you accommodate students and staff with disabilities. It offers data collection strategies, intervention models for difficult students, service review techniques, and more.

disabilitycomplianceforhighereducation.com

Dean & Provost

12 issues for $225 (print) / $180 (e)

From budgeting to faculty tenure and from distance learning to labor relations, *Dean & Provost* gives you innovative ways to manage the challenges of leading your institution. Learn how to best use limited resources, safeguard your institution from frivolous lawsuits, and more.

deanandprovost.com

Enrollment Management Report

12 issues for $230 (print) / $185 (e)

Find out which enrollment strategies are working for your colleagues, which aren't, and why. This publication gives you practical guidance on all aspects—including records, registration, recruitment, orientation, admissions, retention, and more.

enrollmentmanagementreport.com

WANT TO SUBSCRIBE?
Go online or call: 888.378.2537.

JB JOSSEY-BASS
A Wiley Brand